VISIONS OF NOSTRADAMUS AND OTHER PROPHETS

Donald Wigal, Ph.D.

Ottenheimer
PUBLISHERS

Created and manufactured by Ottenheimer Publishers, Inc.
© 1998 Ottenheimer Publishers, Inc.
5 Park Center Court, Suite 300
Owings Mills, Maryland 21117-5001 USA
Printed in the United States of America.
RE987M L K J I H G F E D C B A

ISBN 0-8241-0231-2

To all friends of
The Louise Wigal Memorial Fund

Table of Contents

TIMELINE OF PROPHECY

INTRODUCTION

You are about to meet two dozen or so fascinating people. Most lived centuries ago, yet their insights are amazingly relevant to our understanding of the present and future.

The men and women described here in this book are prophets, seers, and visionaries who seem to have possessed an extraordinary ability to tap into the future and share what they saw. Yet at the same time, these profiles show them to be real human beings, in most ways like the rest of us, who worked, loved, suffered, rejoiced, and sometimes doubted the paths they took.

They were exceptional, however, in their ability to interpret patterns in history. From them we may learn how to make better use of our own insights and intuitions.

Prophets

For most people, the word *prophet* brings to mind the men and women who spoke for a deity through the scriptures of various religions. The Bible Prophets chapter briefly touches on some of these prophets from the Judeo-Christian tradition, concentrating on the major and minor prophets of the Old Testament. However, there have also been many secular prophets throughout history who have gleaned details of the future with no divine inspiration. Others were unsure where their insights came from; they only knew that they were very powerful and undeniable. The majority of this book deals with these secular prophets.

Secular Prophets

Though most people are familiar with Nostradamus, he is only one of the many important prophets profiled in this book. While the term "prophet" is used loosely to describe most of these individuals, they have also been called seers, soothsayers, visionaries, prognosticators, or other terms—as if they all mean the same thing. But there are differences. A seer usually refers to a person who foresees or foretells. At least two of our subjects, Andrew Jackson Davis and Kenneth Mackenzie, are often called seers. A woman prophet falling in this category might be called a seeress, although this term most often is used to describe witches who make prophecies. And although soothsayer is often used as a derogatory term by critics, ironically, it actually means "one who speaks the truth." Visionaries are prophets who not only speak of the future but add creative touches to their predictions that can elevate them from the mundane to the profound. However, writers and other artists may also be called visionaries without claiming to foretell. Leonardo da Vinci and Jules Verne were certainly visionaries.

Most of these individuals were said to have a sixth sense. A person who has this extra sense perceives on another plane that goes beyond sight, smell, taste, touch, or hearing. Some claim they are clairvoyant—able to see what is happening elsewhere. Others are telepathic; they can send and receive messages using only their minds. Prophets are said to be pre-cognitive—they can foretell the future. Others are considered retrocognitive—actually able to see past events as if they are occurring in the present moment. Some may have more than one of these abilities. American visionaries Andrew Jackson Davis and Edgar Cayce could both predict the future and heal telepathically. Others were focused on different talents at different periods of their lives.

There are nearly as many specific ways in which these individuals received their visions and shared them with others as there are prophets. But each had a special openness to the possible—and the unexplainable. They all were able to access the "Eternal Now"; they were attuned to the reality not only that something did happen or is happening, but also could—or will—happen.

Chronologically, our survey begins with the ingenious Leonardo da Vinci, then introduces the remarkable physician Nostradamus, followed by brilliant academic John Dee, ill-fated Kenneth Mackenzie, phenomenal healing clairvoyants Andrew Jackson Davis and Edgar Cayce, prolific writer Jules Verne, celebrated astrologer Evangeline Adams, popular Sun Sign columnist Jeane Dixon, and the highly successful contemporary intuitive Alan Vaughan. People who influenced these prophets' lives or who shared their amazing views of the future are also included on this "journey."

Are these prophets for real? Nostradamus fans point to how easily his writings fit specific events that he seems to have foreseen. His critics point to the ambiguities and inconsistencies in much of his work. As with the predictions of other prophets considered here, those of Nostradamus were apparently only occasionally on target. But, like an audience watching a singing dog, we marvel not at how often or how well a feat is performed, but that it is performed at all.

Prophecy is typically met with skepticism or disbelief, as is the paranormal in general. However, people of each era or place often accept as religion what another time and place may reject as superstition. Prophets are accepted very differently throughout history, depending a great deal on what the people currently in power consider to be, on the one hand, unacceptable superstition and magic, or, on the other, believable revelation and religion.

Following in the bloody footsteps of religious martyrs, some of our secular prophets also suffered greatly for their beliefs. Nostradamus, Dee, Adams, and Cayce were arrested. Mackenzie was tortured and murdered.

At one end of the credibility spectrum, skeptics will never be satisfied because only science and reason make believers out of them. Fanatics at the other extreme, however, appear gullible, as they often accept the most outrageous claims without proof of any kind. This book attempts to present a balanced point of view, so you can find your personal comfort zone when it comes to prophecy. You may also learn to perceive in a revealing new way, and then better envision how your insights relate to the future. For many of us, being open to all things authentically spiritual can only make us wiser.

LEONARDO DA VINCI
The Ultimate Renaissance Man
1452–1519

*Oh! speculators on things, boast not of knowing the things
that nature ordinarily brings about, but rejoice if you
know the end of those things which you yourself devise.*

— Leonardo da Vinci. *Notebooks.* (c. 1500)
Translated by Jean Paul Richter.

Although nearly every country has had its period of
"reawakening," no other place experienced a more
remarkable cultural rebirth than Italy in the fifteenth
century. The French word for this kind of cultural rebirth,
renaissance, was given to that period of major artistic revival,
inspired by the rediscovery of the art and literature of ancient
Greece and Rome.

The Renaissance produced a remarkable number of great
thinkers and artists, including the philosopher and statesman
Machiavelli, the astronomer Copernicus, the painter Raphael,
and the sculptor Michelangelo. But no one from that period

could boast a more impressive and varied list of achievements than Leonardo da Vinci, the ultimate Renaissance man.

Even by Renaissance standards, which called for artists and scientists to master many disciplines, Leonardo was an exceptional person. Many of the nineteenth- and twentieth-century prophets profiled in this book lived longer than his sixty-eight years, but none achieved more. Leonardo, the foremost creative mind of his time—if not of all time—was a painter, scientist, ecologist, anatomist, architect, military engineer, civil engineer, mathematician, musician, author, town planner, theater set designer, and inventor. In all of these areas, he produced work that influenced his era and all generations to come. Though we think of Leonardo mostly as a painter, his incredible mind devised technological wonders that would become part of our lives centuries after his death.

An Artist's Awakening

Leonardo was born in the little town of Vinci, near Florence, in 1452. Born out of wedlock to a wealthy married Florentine man and a peasant girl, Leonardo was brought up by his father, who convinced the boy's natural mother that the child would be better off with him and his wife. Biographer Giorgio Vasari wrote that from his earliest childhood, Leonardo was known to doodle drawings of futuristic machines to pass the time. He also displayed artistic, musical, and mathematical talent as a child. Leonardo's father sent him to Florence at the age of fifteen to apprentice to a great painter, Verrocchio. It was here that the young boy learned both painting and the mechanical arts. Leonardo quickly became Verrocchio's most promising pupil, and soon everyone in Florence—the center of the Renaissance—was talking about the handsome and personable young man who had already painted a number of innovative masterpieces, one of which was *The Adoration of the Magi.*

But Leonardo's restless mind drove him to explore other areas, too. In 1482, he moved to Milan to pursue a variety of projects. Although he painted such masterpieces as *The Last Supper* during this period, he also acted as a military and architectural advisor to the Duke of Milan. He began his investigations into science, combining his keen ability to observe the natural world with his artistic expertise to produce remarkable sketches of everything and everyone around him. He recorded his thoughts and drawings in notebooks, which would not be discovered by the rest of the world until long after his death. Consisting of thousands and thousands of pages of drawings and text, the notebooks contain a dazzling array of insights and inventions that were centuries ahead of their time. Filled with drawings of vehicles resembling submarines, military tanks, automobiles (horseless carriages), and helicopters, his journals seemed to have been written on a journey into the future.

Ruth Saunders Magurn, in her profile of Leonardo for Funk & Wagnall's *New Encyclopedia* (1973), has remarked that "had his notebooks been published they would have revolutionized the science of his day.... Leonardo had actually anticipated much of the science of modern times."

A Jack of All Trades

During the middle years of his life, Leonardo moved restlessly between Milan and Florence, working briefly in the early 1500s as senior military architect and general engineer for the notorious Cesare Borgia, a powerful Renaissance warrior. Borgia was well aware of Leonardo's genius, and wanted the artist to help him build a city of the future. Leonardo's groundbreaking work in cartography, anatomy, hydraulic engineering, and geology left him little time for painting, and he began many artistic projects only to abandon them. He did, however, produce his great masterpiece, *Mona Lisa* (1503–1506), during this time.

As Leonardo grew older, he nearly abandoned painting altogether, and concentrated mostly on his scientific explorations. At the age of sixty-five, he left Italy forever to become "first painter and architect and engineer" for the new King of France, Francis I. He spent most of his last years inventing amusements for the king, such as a mechanical walking lion. He died in France in 1519.

Visionary

Leonardo's innovations in nearly all of his endeavors have prompted some people to wonder whether he could see into the future. But unlike most of the prophets we will consider here, Leonardo was a "seer" strictly in the literal sense of the word. For him, sight was the key to all knowledge, and his great powers of observation, combined with a thirst for knowledge and an extraordinary imagination, allowed him to penetrate mysteries that others hardly dreamed of. He thought that seeing things clearly was the way to understand how the world worked, and his lifelong desire to observe and record everything he saw led to works that, in hindsight, seem amazingly prophetic.

Leonardo's uncanny powers of observation are most apparent in his art. As a painter he was an expert draftsman, colorist, and inventor of the *sfumato*, or smoky, style of painting, in which extremely subtle shading was achieved through barely visible transitions between colors. This technique, along with his innovations in showing atmospheric perspective, conveying motion, and grouping figures, influenced painters at least a hundred years after his death. Leonardo's *Treatise on Painting*, written between 1485 and 1500, is still considered a major resource for artists today. In it, he boldly set forth his belief that painters, with their ability to perceive and re-create the world, are the people most qualified to achieve and convey knowledge of all things.

Set designer

Leonardo's ingenious innovations in set design earned him a place in the history of theater. He constructed revolving scenery in 1490, although an actual revolving stage did not come into use until Karl Lautenschlager in Munich invented the electrically operated turntable in 1896. According to Margot Berthold's *A History of World Theater* (1972), for one festival Leonardo designed a movable planetary system, picturesque costumes for actors portraying gods and goddesses, masks representing savages, and "fantastic fabulous beasts."

A collaborator with Leonardo on a festival at Milan described one of their stage decorations: The festival play was called *Paradiso* because, "By the great gift of invention and the art of Master Leonardo da Vinci of Florence, there was constructed Paradise with all the seven planets, and it turned in a circle. . . ."

Sculptor

Leonardo's great gifts as a sculptor were never realized, but the sketches of unfinished projects he left behind suggest monumental works of great skill and beauty. He labored for years on a bronze equestrian statue that, had it been completed, would have measured sixteen feet high—double the size of any in existence at that time.

Engineer and cartographer

Aside from his gifts as an artist, Leonardo's genius helped him devise innovations that have practical value to this day. For example, after his first stay in Milan, Leonardo returned to Florence in 1503, where he devised a plan to build a large canal that would connect Florence with the sea. Although the scheme was never carried out, it provided an excellent model of canal engineering that is still in use. Interestingly, the express highway that connects Florence to the sea today travels over the exact route of Leonardo's proposed canal.

Similarly, Leonardo's expeditions for his employer, Cesare Borgia, resulted in striking changes in cartography, or mapmaking. For example, he created bird's-eye views of towns that reproduced in miniature the actual spatial dimensions of the landscape onto a sheet of paper, a technique commonly used today.

The Notebooks

Although Leonardo was renowned for numerous talents, it is through the prophetic ideas and inventions he set down in his notebooks, undiscovered until centuries after his death, that we get a true picture of the scope of his genius. These records, unknown until the first was published in 1881, contain detailed plans, sketches, and drawings for many machines that were later invented (many still in use today, such as the crankshaft and the spring motors in clocks). He also filled pages with intricate anatomical studies that predate our modern medical understanding of the human body. And his elaborate studies of nature are at the root of modern geophysical, botanical, hydrological, and aerological knowledge.

Begun during his first stay in Milan, the notebooks were Leonardo's attempt to catalogue and understand the observable world. He had hoped to publish his scientific research in the same way as was his *Treatise on Painting*, but this was not to happen in his lifetime.

Much has been made of the fact that Leonardo wrote in the notebooks using a backwards script that can only be deciphered by holding it before a mirror. Was he purposely trying to disguise his ideas? Actually, it may simply be that, being left-handed, Leonardo found it easier to write that way. We probably will never know the answer to this puzzle.

In all, thirty-one of Leonardo's notebooks survived, two of which were discovered as recently as 1965. Groups of notebooks are housed in libraries all over Europe, and one collection, called the Codex Leicester, was recently bought at auction by Microsoft chairman and twentieth-century innovator Bill Gates for $30.8 million. It is possible that even more notebooks and papers remain undiscovered; and that the full magnitude of Leonardo's genius has not yet been realized.

Genius in motion

In these notebooks, Leonardo described his explorations into almost every area of the natural world, and he predicted discoveries in several branches of science. He was fascinated by motion, particularly the movement of water, air currents, the flight of birds, and the nature of sound waves. He pondered the interaction of land and water and the formation of fossils as a way to understand the history of the earth, much as modern geologists and paleontologists do today.

In the early 1500s, Leonardo discovered the effect of the moon upon the tides, anticipating today's understanding of how continents formed. He also wondered if the tides were moved by the sun and the moon, or by "the breathing of a terrestrial machine," as he wrote in his notebook. In fact, he hypothesized that the earth was like a breathing body, its rivers like human veins. As primitive as this view may seem today, it was an advance in scientific speculation. One of his biographers, Roger Whiting, points out that Leonardo "used this theory to oppose medievalists who argued that the oceans' surfaces rise at their centers higher than necessary to activate mountain springs."

Leonardo's analogy between the earth's circulatory process and that of the human body was typical of his desire to discover an ordered system of relationships among all things. Just as water circulates around the earth, he believed human blood circulates through the body and courses through the veins in much the same way. His findings deepened our understanding of the circulatory system. For Leonardo, the human body was a model for understanding the design of the universe as well as the earth. He even related his design for an ideal church to the dome of the human skull.

Flying machines

Just as he saw connections between the human body, the earth, and the universe, Leonardo observed the flight of birds and wondered why people could not fly, too. Of all the prophetic inventions he recorded in the notebooks, Leonardo's experiments with flying machines fascinate contemporary admirers most.

Shortly before he wrote a "Design for a Flying Machine" in 1488, Leonardo secretly created a model airplane designed along the lines of the wings of bats. His descriptions and illustrations show several design elements, such as retractable flaps, which were later actually used in airplanes. It wasn't until more than 350 years after Leonardo's experiments, in 1852, that the first man-carrying glider was built by Sir George Cayley in Yorkshire, England. The following year, Cayley's coachman made the first true manned flight.

Between 1514 and 1519, Leonardo wrote *Studies of the Anatomy of a Bird's Wing and Bird Flight*. His studies and experiments in human anatomy, especially in the area of musculature, led him to conclude that it was impossible for man to successfully imitate the flight of birds. But Leonardo then proposed mechanical alternatives, including a plan for a "flying screw," which resembled the basic principle of a helicopter's propeller.

Along with his notes on the "flying screw," Leonardo made an entry in one of his notebooks regarding what we now call a parachute: "If a man has a tent made of linen of which the apertures have all been stopped up . . . he will be able to throw himself down from any great height without sustaining any injury." Similarly, Leonardo referred to a device like a life preserver, suggesting that when his flying machine is "tried over a lake . . . you should carry a big wine-skin as a girdle so that in case you fall in you will not be drowned."

The Legacy of Leonardo

Throughout his life, Leonardo da Vinci was plagued by a sense of failure and frustration that he left so many projects unfinished, and that his work could never match the perfection of nature. Only in modern times are people able to appreciate the scope and accuracy of his visions, and how close to that perfection he actually came. Today, we recognize the truly extraordinary nature of his achievements in a way that was impossible for people to understand during his lifetime. Consequently, excitement over Leonardo's contributions—not only to art but also to other realms such as science, medicine, and aeronautics—is building. During the time this book was being written, for example, plays based on his notebooks and his life were being produced, countless computer web sites celebrated his accomplishments, curators at a science museum in Italy had created full-scale models of his mechanical inventions, and his Leicester Codex was on an around-the-world tour. Clearly, this Renaissance visionary was generating excitement at a level that even Leonardo—the great seer—could not have predicted.

NOSTRADAMUS
The Most Famous Prophet
1503–1566

*I fear that these calculations might be welcomed more by
laughter than by admiration.*

— Nostradamus, in a letter to Lorenz Tubbe, 1561

With his long, flowing beard and piercing eyes, no
one conjures up the image of a prophet quite like
Nostradamus, sixteenth-century astrologer, physician, poet, and mystic. Almost everyone has at least heard of
him, and his writings are studied seriously by scholars to this
day. Why has Nostradamus captured the imaginations of so
many, for so many generations? Although for much of his
life he was regarded simply as a well-respected doctor, the
stories surrounding him are steeped in the macabre. Take
this tale from the crypt:

Legend has it that in the year 1700, grave robbers opened
Nostradamus's tomb and were horrified to find the seer's
skeleton adorned with a metal medallion engraved with the
letters MDCC—the Latin equivalent of 1700! (Francis X.

King, *Nostradamus*, 1994). Did Nostradamus predict the year his grave would be vandalized?

Like many of Nostradamus's famous writings, this story has been interpreted many ways. This is the version according to the *Encyclopedia of Witches and Witchcraft* (Rosemary Ellen Guiley, ed., 1989):

> In 1791 . . . three superstitious soldiers opened his grave. . . . The soldiers were intent on testing a story that whoever drank from the skull of Nostradamus would inherit his prophetic powers. They were unmindful of another story that whoever disturbed the grave would [soon] die. When the grave was opened, the soldiers were amazed to see a plaque that read 1791 hung around the neck of the skeleton, as though Nostradamus had predicted the year his grave would be violated. One of the men poured wine into the skull and drank from it—and was subsequently shot dead by a stray bullet from nearby fighting.

These stories and others like them reflect some of the never-ending fascination surrounding Nostradamus. Many are familiar with his ties to the occult and his more popular predictions that seem to defy all chance of coincidence. But few know the man behind the mystery. In actuality he was a gifted doctor who led a rich and full life, long before he put pen to paper to record the visions that would make him forever synonymous with the word "prophecy."

The World's Most Famous Prophet

More than four hundred books and essays about the Nostradamus prophecies have been written, as well as many articles and commentaries in several languages. Currently, the word *Nostradamus* brings up hundreds of links in just one of a dozen on-line Internet search engines. Commercial films about Nostradamus include *The Man Who Saw Tomorrow*, produced by Warner Brothers in 1981. Yet he is not included in most standard encyclopedias or cultural literacy dictionaries. Most likely he will always remain a subject of great controversy, ridiculed by some and revered by others.

Skeptics say that Nostradamus's puzzling predictions are meaningless, while fanatics claim that he consistently and accurately foresaw events far into the future. But even his most severe critics acknowledge that Nostradamus was an ingenious and courageous physician and a skilled writer.

Nostradamus achieved fame, if not fortune, during his own lifetime; first for his medical achievements, and later for his published works. Eventually, he became an international sensation because of his predictions. There is no question that many people in positions of power throughout history consulted the man and his writings, hoping to shed light on their fates. In Nostradamus's own day, he was a favorite of the court, regularly consulted by his queen, Catherine de Medici. Reportedly, World War II leaders from both sides used his writings in their propaganda as evidence of sure victory to come.

Unlike the other prophets profiled here, there are no known manuscripts in Nostradamus's own handwriting. Also, we have no authentic documentation of the amazing feats attributed to him. Yet, through the ages, the portrait that emerges of this man is a vivid one, with all the elements of an epic Hollywood movie. From his heroic days curing plague victims to his desperate wanderings following the tragic deaths of his wife and children, to his final days devoted to recording frequent visions, his life was one of extreme highs and lows.

The Man

Michel de Nostradame was born in France early in 1503, bridging the period between fellow prophets Leonardo da Vinci in the fifteenth century and John Dee later in the sixteenth century. At some point in his life, Michel began to use the Latin form of his family name, Nostradamus. Over time, he came to be known by this name alone.

Nostradamus was the first of five sons born of educated Jewish parents who publicly converted to Catholicism, but continued to practice Judaism in private. Jews at the time often did this to avoid persecution by the Inquisition. This is important in understanding Nostradamus, because at one point he was a student of the Kabbalah (or Cabala), a mystical Jewish philisophy or system of interpreting the Scriptures that also influenced prophet John Dee. The Kabbalah is based on the belief that every word, letter, number, and accent of the Five Books of Moses has a secret meaning, contains mysteries, and therefore can be used in magical practices or secret rites.

Schooling a visionary

By most accounts Nostradamus was a precocious boy who received an intensive, home-based education. He received his first taste of the occult, as well as a broad traditional education, from his two grandfathers. These learned men, who were friends, were astrologers and physicians known for their psychic powers. They also were thought to have been advisors to the French royal court. Reportedly, they passed on to Nostradamus ancient Persian and Egyptian books on astrology, which he memorized and then burned. From them he also learned Latin, Greek, Hebrew, mathematics, and astronomy. He later went on to study liberal arts at the University of Avignon and then enrolled at the University of Montpellier to study medicine.

While attending these schools, Nostradamus was said to have entertained his fellow students with his surprising scientific views, including his belief that the earth revolved around the sun. He was not the first to believe this—astronomer Nicholas Copernicus (1473–1543) first developed the idea. But this was an unpopular notion at that time, to say the least.

Despite his controversial beliefs, Nostradamus soon was recognized for his healing skill. At a young age he was allowed to treat patients and enjoyed considerable success, especially in treating victims of the Black Plague in southern France. However, many physicians objected to his original and unorthodox cures. He refused to "bleed" patients, for example, which was a common practice as late as the nineteenth century. He also was also a firm believer in the powers of fresh air and sterilized water—both unusual ideas then. It could be that his refusal to practice the violent and intrusive methods of healing popular at the time, such as bleeding and purging, was the secret to his success as a doctor. Surely patients already weakened by the plague did not benefit from those sorts of cures.

After making a name for himself treating plague victims, Nostradamus returned to Montpellier and earned his medical degree. When he was about thirty, he moved to Agen. He did so in part at the urging of a new friend, Jules Cesar Scaliger, a multi-talented academic and astrologer known for his abrasive personality. Many believe it was Scaliger who introduced Nostradamus to the art of prophecy. Scholars also believe it might have been Scaliger's more disreputable deeds that made the members of the court of the Inquisition take notice of Nostradamus.

Nostradamus married soon afterward, and the couple had two children. Tragically, his extraordinary medical knowledge could not save his own family—his wife and children all died of a plague-like illness. As a widower, he began his bleakest period. And, adding to his suffering, his wife's family even sued him to get her dowry back.

On the run

It was at about this time that Nostradamus ran into an artist friend who was working on a statue of the Virgin Mary.

Nostradamus told the sculptor that it looked as though he was casting a statue of the devil. Though he claimed he was only trying to tell his friend it wasn't very good, someone who heard the remark was not amused, and Nostradamus was charged with heresy. The 1500s was not a century when one could afford to be casual about such matters. At about the same time his medical practice failed and he had a falling-out with Scaliger. Then, to add to his miseries, he received warnings that authorities of the Inquisition, or ecclesiastical court, wanted to question him. To escape his troubles, Nostradamus left Agen to wander around Europe for more than six years.

The Inquisition had a profound effect on Nostradamus's life and works. This judgmental body was established by the hierarchy of the Catholic Church in the twelfth century to prosecute cases of heresy. Once convicted, victims of the Inquisition were handed over to the civil authorities for punishment, which often included execution. Persecution of individuals the court believed to be seers, witches, fortune-tellers, and the like was not unusual. It was a time of witch-hunts in France, and those who healed in unorthodox ways were frequently targets.

A force for good

Inquisition authorities were not alone in thinking that Nostradamus's powers were derived from dabbling in the occult. The seer himself said that throughout his life, he experienced visions that gradually increased in frequency and intensity, until he himself thought he might be possessed by evil spirits. Sometime between losing his family and remarrying, he retreated to an abbey, where he lived as a monk. There, he discussed his visions with the abbot. In that prayerful environment, Nostradamus decided that his gift was a positive—not a diabolical—vocation. From then on he believed he had inherited the powers of prophecy that both his grandfathers had claimed.

The Hero

Nostradamus went from the abbey to Marseilles, where again he successfully treated plague victims. Town authorities were so grateful they gave him a large sum of money. However, Nostradamus gave the money back to the widows and orphans of the plague victims. He was not a greedy man; he seemed only to want to live comfortably enough to be able to tell the world about his dramatic predictions.

Also during this time, while he traveled around Europe, Nostradamus met many physicians, astrologers, and other thinkers who contributed to his enthusiasm for the occult. During this period, stories of his clairvoyance began to accumulate, contributing to his growing reputation as a visionary.

In 1547, in his mid-forties, Nostradamus took as his second wife a wealthy and well-connected widow and settled in Salon de Craux, where he came to be known as the "Seer of Salon." Here, among other things, he made cosmetics for the very wealthy, but soon came to spend more and more time studying and practicing magic and astrology. He fathered six more children, even while traveling extensively and successfully combating the plague in several cities. Having married into money, he was able to devote himself to what was becoming his true calling—foretelling the future.

Gazing into the Beyond

Nostradamus experienced his visions nightly during scrying sessions. (The art of scrying is described in more detail in the upcoming chapter on John Dee.) In simple terms, scrying could be compared to a kind of self-hypnosis during which clairvoyants see visions on the surface of an object. Though crystal balls are probably the most commonly known scrying device, Nostradamus's own method involved gazing into a bowl of water. He also, at times, incorporated into these sessions magical rites attributed to the ancient Greek oracles of Branchus.

Nostradamus himself claimed that his visions for the future came to him through a mixture of divine inspiration, magic, and clairvoyance. He described his technique in his writings:

> Sitting in secret study at night,
> Alone upon the brass tripod
> A slight flame comes out of the solitude
> With a promise of magic which may be believed.

> With rod in hand set in the midst of the branches,
> With water he moistens both the fringe and the foot.
> Fear, and a voice make me quake in my sleeves:
> Divine splendor, the God is seated nearby.

Prolific Prophet

In 1550, Nostradamus issued the first of his annual almanacs. These astrological pamphlets forecasting events for the coming year were a popular form of literature at the time. While Nostradamus wasn't the only one writing them, inasmuch as his almanacs were quickly translated into English, they appear to have had widespread appeal. Then, in 1555, he published the first group of his *Centuries*, writings upon which his reputation is based today.

In this case, the term *Centuries* refers to groups of stanzas called "quatrains" and not to a period of one hundred years. Eventually Nostradamus wrote more than a thousand quatrains. These writings appear to predict events from about 1560 to the end of time. Remarkably, they were almost immediately in demand, though their meanings were so obscure almost no one could make sense of them. However, there have always been, and probably always will be, those people who insist that certain of Nostradamus's words and phrases match world events or their own experiences so closely that he must truly have been clairvoyant.

Around 1555, after his first group of prophecies had been published, Nostradamus received the endorsement of Catherine de Medici (1519–1588), the very powerful queen who influenced both church and state during the reigns of at least ten consecutive popes, and who had four popes as relatives.

From friars to kings

Along with his writings, Nostradamus was known for a more direct kind of prophesying: He told people what he thought would happen to them. Chavigny, a dedicated pupil of Nostradamus's who was to become the seer's first biographer, is most likely responsible for spreading the following story, which is retold by Roger Fadness in *Peoples Almanac #2* (Doubleday-Dell, 1978).

> While in Italy, Nostradamus encountered a party of Franciscan friars. He walked up to one of them, a young man named Felice Peretti, and knelt before him. When questioned about his behavior, Nostradamus replied, 'I must kneel before His holiness.' After the death of Pope Gregory XIII, Peretti was elected [Pope] Sixtus V in 1585, nineteen years after Nostradamus's death.

Another tale of Nostradamus's second sight goes that while Nostradamus was a guest at the chateau of the Seigneur de Florinville in Lorraine, his host challenged him to foretell the future of two pigs, one black and one white.

"You will eat the black one, a wolf will consume the other," Nostradamus reportedly said. In an effort to prove him wrong, de Florinville ordered the white pig to be slaughtered and prepared for that night's feast. After the host and guest had dined, de Florinville boasted of his victory, but the seer insisted his prediction had indeed come true. The nobleman called in the cook to settle the dispute, and was amazed when the chef admitted that a wolf cub had snuck in the kitchen and had eaten the white pig. Not seeing what difference it made, the chef had cooked the black one instead.

Besides casting horoscopes at court and foretelling the future, Nostradamus also told fortunes by reading the moles on a person's body, a form of divination popular at the time. Though it may be viewed as odd that a physician, who is supposed to be scientific by nature, would dabble in the occult, this is not so strange as it may seem. Throughout history, it has not been unusual for physicians to practice astrology and other occult rituals. Even today, homeopathic and other health-care practitioners may call on astrology for insight.

The prediction that brought Nostradamus international attention was one that came to be associated with the death of King Henry II. Nostradamus wrote a quatrain about an old lion killed on a warlike field by "one of two piercings" (see Notable Predictions, page 28). When, six years later, Henry was killed during a jousting tournament by the younger Montgomery, captain of the Scottish guard, Catherine de Medici was convinced that Nostradamus had made a powerful and accurate prediction. So convinced, in fact, that she eventually appointed him court physician under the reign of Henry's successor, his son Charles IX. (It is interesting to note that she rewarded him for this prediction of tragedy, rather than accusing him of sorcery or another crime, as was the case with Kenneth Mackenzie and some of the other prophets profiled later in this book.) Nostradamus lived at the royal court in Paris at the queen's invitation until illness forced him to return to Salon.

When the queen invited him to her court in 1556, the seer was fifty-three and she was thirty-seven. It was rumored that he may have been her lover, despite the fact that he was married and suffered from various conditions including arthritis, gout, and dropsy. Catherine reportedly traveled at least once to see Nostradamus in Salon. Whether or not these tales were true, being a close advisor to the queen was a great honor. This association most likely had a great deal to do with the public's acceptance of Nostradamus's published works during his own lifetime. While he was in Paris, most of Parisian society declared him a genius, probably even divinely inspired. Others considered him at best a fake—and at worst—a sorcerer. Perceptions of the man and his prophecies were strongly divided. Then, as now, he was a controversial figure.

Predicting his own death

After suffering poor health for some time, Nostradamus wrote his will. He arranged to be buried standing up, supposedly so the people of Salon would not walk upon his body as it lay buried. On July 1, 1566, he asked a priest to give him the Church's last rites. The great prophet was found dead at his workbench the next morning. Chavigny, his devoted pupil, recalled that Nostradamus had said, "Tomorrow at sunrise I shall not be here."

His epitaph, written by his second wife, reads: "Here lie the bones of the illustrious Michel Nostradamus, who alone of all mortals was judged worthy to record with almost divine pen, under the influence of the stars, the future of the entire world."

Together with Nostradamus's widow, Chavigny helped publish what is considered a definitive version of Nostradamus's prophecies, thus ensuring the master a place in history.

The Nostradamus Legacy

In 1781, long after the prophet's death, Pope Pius VI shunned the writings of Nostradamus but not the man himself. The writings were added to the *Index Librorum Prohibitorum*, or *Index of Forbidden Books*. The *Index* was virtually abolished in 1966 after the Second Vatican Council (1962–1965).

The Centuries

During his lifetime and today, part of the fascination surrounding Nostradamus is based on just how difficult it is to decipher his writings. As mentioned earlier, Nostradamus wrote his prophecies in rhymed four-line verses called quatrains. He then organized these verses into groups of about one hundred each, calling each group a *Century*. In his day they were known as *Les Prophéties*.

The first edition, published in 1555, contained 354 quatrains. An expanded edition of the *Centuries* was published three years after the first. Altogether, Nostradamus completed nine centuries, numbered one through six, and eight through ten. For some reason he left out the seventh. He died before finishing the eleventh and twelfth *Centuries*.

Nearly every quatrain is presumed to have one or more applications to some historical event, past or future. The seer's followers, or Nostradamians, believe these strange writings to be not only plausible but accurate down to the minutest detail. Based on these quatrains, Nostradamus has been credited with predicting, among other things, the Great Fire of London; the French Revolution; the toppling or deaths of monarchs, popes, and other world leaders; aerial and nuclear warfare; communism; and even the Kennedy family tragedies. Like many of the prophets profiled here, he also envisioned rockets ("machines of flying fire") and submarines ("iron fish" to be used for warfare).

With only a quick glance at these writings, it is easy to see why some dismiss Nostradamus as a quack. Peppered with an odd hodgepodge of modern and archaic languages, anagrams, invented words, and other forms of word play, they range from the almost indecipherable to the very specific, which include dates and place names. In a preface to the first edition of the *Centuries*, written in the form of a letter to his son, César, Nostradamus himself wrote that he had for a time withheld his predictions, out of fear of public condemnation. He later changed his mind. "But later on I thought I would for the common good describe the most important of the revolutionary changes I foresee, but that so as not to upset my present readers I would do this in a cloudy manner with abstruse and twisted sentences rather than plainly prophetical." He believed, too, that the meaning of his verses would become clear only after an incident had taken place.

Some commentaries say Nostradamus wrote this way in order to make his meaning less obvious to the Inquisition witch-hunters, who were trying to convict him of sorcery. However, church and civil experts were able to understand the languages he used. More likely, he intended to add mystery and possibly entertainment value to his prophecies, as well as to leave the window open to many interpretations. In any case, his confusing lines certainly enhanced his image as a prophet and inspired respect in some circles. This was a time when, as the philosopher Montaigne (1533–1592) wrote, "Nothing is so firmly believed as what is least known."

However, for each neatly worked-out solution to one of the seer's puzzles, there are skeptics who ridicule it. It seems the only sure thing when it comes to prophecy is that there is no sure thing.

The problems of (mis)interpretation

Each line of Nostradamus's quatrains has ten beats, with a pause after the fourth beat and an accent on the fifth beat. When translated, these quatrains typically lose either their original meter, their meaning, or both. The task of interpreting Nostradamus's *Centuries* has been rendered even more difficult because of what has been done to them over the years. The magician James Randi points out a problem similar to one that historians encounter when they study published manuscripts in general, from scripture to contemporary journals. "Typographical errors, transpositions, changed italicization, punctuation and capitalization, altered spellings, and 'improvements' on Nostradamus's writings have bastardized his works to the point where proper scholarship is difficult." Moreover, he said, "There is no ideal version of Nostradamus's works. . . ."

Interestingly, Nostradamus did not set down his predictions in any kind of chronological order, almost as if to add to the puzzle. Perhaps some quatrains actually refer to *past* events. One of the advantages of this ambiguity is that any quatrain may apply to both a past and a future event.

Notable Predictions

The following are the events and writings most often cited as proof-positive of Nostradamus's second sight. However, because his language is so vague, it is virtually impossible to prove that his words mean one thing or another. The genius of Nostradamus may have been his ability to write verses with such universal appeal that people of all ages and all cultures can relate to them and make them fit their own views.

Henry II's death (1559)

The apparent fulfillment of Century I, Quatrain 35, is said to be what made Nostradamus internationally famous in his own day. However, the critics build an impressive case against its accuracy.

Century I, Quatrain 35
The young Lion shall overcome the old
On a warlike field in single combat,

He will pierce his eyes in a cage of gold,
One of two breakings, then he shall die a cruel death.

After the actual 1559 event to which this prophecy is usually applied, "the young Lion" of the quatrain was taken to refer to Montgomery, a commander of the Scottish Guards, whose broken lance killed King Henry II during a jousting match. Both jousters supposedly wore shields emblazoned with a lion's head.

The usual interpretation of Century I, Quatrain 35 by Nostradamians is that Montgomery was the "young lion" matched against the "old" king. But critics point out that the six-year age difference between Montgomery and the king was not really significant enough to differentiate them as "young" and "old."

Believers say "single combat" referred to the jousting tournament. At that time in jousting, men on horseback charged at each other with long lances. The "cage of gold" is often thought to mean the gilded visor the king wore. Montgomery's lance broke and part of it entered the king's eye through his visor, mortally wounding him. "One of two breakings" is sometimes taken to refer to a broken lance, or to the second of two charges at the king, or even to two wounds caused by the lance's entrance and presumed exit from the king's body.

One interesting note: In the sixteenth century, armor for both horse and rider was virtually indestructible. Usually, the only way to disable a knight was to knock him off his horse. In the accident that killed Henry II, however, Montgomery's lance broke and then was able to enter first the helmet and then the king's eye. This rare occurrence does seem to bear a strong resemblance to Nostradamus's pierced cage. But again, translation is everything. Other versions of the quatrain cite the second line as "On a field of war," which critics say hardly matches a jousting tournament.

Great Fire of London (1666)

Those who believe Nostradamus predicted this event base their confidence on the following:

Century II, Quatrain 51
The blood of the just shall be required of London,
Burned by fire in thrice twenty and six.
The ancient Dame shall fall from her high place,
And many of the same sect shall fall.

In 1666, a terrible fire began in a bakery and raged for many days, destroying much in its path. Some say that by Dame, Nostradamus was referring to Saint Paul's Cathedral. Evidently, the seer frequently used the word "dame" to refer to a church. By "many of the same sect," it is possible that he was referring to the more than eighty churches that burned to the ground during the conflagration.

French Revolution and Napoleonic Wars

Nostradamus, a stout and conservative Catholic, believed in the sanctity of the royal family. Some say he was shocked by, but sure of, the violence and upheaval he saw in the future of the monarchy. Many quatrains have been taken to refer to the period of the French Revolution (1789–1792) and subsequent establishment of the Napoleonic empire (1803–1815), including the following:

Century I, Quatrain 14
Songs, chants, and requests from the
Enslaved people
Shall be received in the future
As divine oracles by headless idiots.

The storming of the Bastille, the uprising of the peasants, and the subsequent beheadings of royalty appear to be a good fit with these stanzas.

Century I, Quatrain 3
When the litter is overturned by the whirlwind
And they will cover their faces with their cloaks,
The republic will be troubled by new people,
Then white and red will judge in opposing ways.

This quatrain is a good example of how eerily specific Nostradamus could be. The beginning of the quatrain could be an apt description of the nobles, who, attempting to flee the city, were literally pulled off their carriages and litters by the angry mob. These nobles often tried to disguise themselves during their escape by hiding their faces with their cloaks. In the last line, "white" could easily be taken to mean the color of the royalists, and red, the color of the revolutionaries.

Some say Nostradamus used an anagram for Napoleon in Century VIII, Quatrain 1 (Pay, Nay, Loron), while others claim the following (Century I, Quatrain 60) refers to Napoleon's reign:

An emperor will be born near Italy
Who will cost the empire very dear.
The people with whom he mixes will say
He will be found less of a prince than a butcher.

While Napoleon was thought to have brought France its first stable government in over a decade, the Napoleonic Wars were devastating to France, resulting in a great number of casualties.

The rise of Hitler
Nostradamus's specific mention of the name Hister, which many take to mean Hitler, has sparked the interest of even the most skeptical over the last fifty years. Scholars of

Nostradamus point to his frequent use of anagrams to refer to people and places, noting that he often replaced a single letter. Skeptics note that the word *hister* was used by the Romans to refer to "river." However, river doesn't make a great deal of sense inserted into the quatrains in question.

Here are two that were so remarkably like actual events that even the Nazis became paranoid.

Century II, Quatrain 24
Beasts wild with hunger will cross rivers.
The greater part of the field will be against Hister.
The great one will be dragged in an iron cage
When the Child of Germany observes nothing.

Century V, Quatrain 94
He will transfer into greater Germany
Brabant and Flanders, Ghent, Bruge, and Boulogne.
The truce, a sham, the great duke of Armenia
Will attack Vienna and Cologne.

The Kennedy assassinations

Fans of Nostradamus throughout the ages have naturally looked to his quatrains for predictions pertaining to their own time. In the modern day, one of the most persistent views held by believers is that Nostradamus predicted the tragic deaths of both John F. and Robert Kennedy (in 1963 and 1968, respectively), in not just one but many quatrains. Here are a few:

Century II, Quatrain 57
Before the conflict the great man will fall,
The lamented great one [will fall] to sudden death,
Born imperfect, he will go the greater part of the way,
Near the river of blood the ground is stained.

Century X, Quatrain 26
The successor will avenge his handsome brother,
And occupy the realm under the shadow of revenge,
He, killed, the obstacle of the guilty dead, his blood.

While parallels can of course be drawn, like many of Nostradamus's quatrains, these lines are so vague they could apply to any number of other people and events.

Other predictions Nostradamians claim have come true include:

✦ American Revolutionary War
✦ American Civil War
✦ Assassination of Abraham Lincoln
✦ Air and space travel
✦ Civil war in Spain caused by "Franco" (Francisco Franco: 1892–1975)
✦ Abdication of Edward VIII
✦ Development of the atomic bomb
✦ Manned rockets to the moon
✦ Rise of the Ayatollah Khomeini

Antichrists

Passages in Nostradamus are interpreted to mean that there would be three Antichrists, each with his or her own reign of terror. Some Nostradamians, apparently believing that dictatorships and war are requirements of such reigns, believe that Napoleon and Hitler were the first two Antichrists. These interpretations inspire books with titles such as *Nostradamus: Countdown to Apocalypse*.

Some believe that Nostradamus predicted that 1998 would be the year the Antichrist somehow gets an "antipope" elected. The likelihood of a papal election in 1998 was taken more seriously in light of the fragile health of John Paul II, who reportedly suffers from a form of Parkinson's disease.

Nostradamus also may have predicted that the Second Coming of Christ would occur in the year 2000. However, he told his son in a letter that the world would end in 3797. To many prophets, the Second Coming does not necessarily mean the end of the world. The Antichrist, the Second

Coming, and end-of-the-world predictions are not always synchronized, but they may overlap in some prophecies.

Some interpret the quatrains as predicting that the third Antichrist, a Middle Eastern tyrant, would, with the assistance of the Soviet Union, start World War III in the late 1990s, beginning with the destruction of New York City. They say that the war will last twenty-seven years before the Antichrist is killed.

Here is the Nostradamus Century X, Quatrain 72, which is taken to refer very ominously to this possibility:

> The year 1999, seven months,
> From the sky will come a great King of Terror:
> To bring back to life the great King of the Mongols,
> Before and after Mars to reign by good luck.

After quoting this, James Randi simply says, "Ho Hum." Nostradamus expert Francis X. King refers to it merely as "the gloomy prediction ... yet to be confirmed."

A Note of Hope

Like many prophets, Nostradamus's predictions tended to be gloomy and to center on cataclysmic or tragic events. He also believed, however, that by keeping their eyes on the horizon, individuals could change their own destinies and even the fate of the world. In his own way, he must have believed he was doing his best to put humankind on the right course.

JOHN DEE

The Scrying Prophet
1527–1608

*I would never attain wisdom by man's hand or by human
power, but only from God, directly or indirectly.*

— John Dee, Preface to *The Enochian Evocation*

I magine a crystal ball. Most people see them in the hands
of gypsy fortune-tellers, who gaze into their depths to
predict handsome dark strangers and long voyages. Yet
one of the most notable crystal-gazing experts of all time was
a fifteenth-century intellectual, court advisor, and "scryer,"
whose advice was sought by royalty.

Less than a decade after the death of Leonardo da Vinci,
Englishman John Dee was born. He would become an extraordinary individual whose intellectual power would eventually
approximate Leonardo's. Like Leonardo and Nostradamus,
Dee was a master of many trades: He was a classical scholar,
professor, mathematician, navigator, cartographer, astronomer,
cleric, theater set designer, healer, alchemist, prolific writer,
and clairvoyant. Often referred to as "Doctor Dee," though

he was neither a physician nor an academic doctor, Dee has been acknowledged by historians as very likely the most learned man in Europe in his day. He was also a rare hybrid, a man of both science and mysticism. This dual nature and his practice of promoting the link between the two make him a forefather of the New Age movement today. Despite the fact that he was revered as one of the great minds of his day in an age of unparalleled genius, Dee's fascination with the occult has led to lingering doubts as to his credibility.

Like Nostradamus, Dee experienced as much misery as success during his lifetime. His guidance was sought by blue bloods and leaders the world over; nonetheless, he died a pauper, after selling portions of his vast library of books one by one for food. How did this man, lauded as a genius, fall so far from grace? In Dee's case, it was not so much *what* he said and did, but the people with whom he chose to associate, which brought about his downfall. He seemed to have a knack for attracting shady business partners who took advantage of him and brought him untold grief.

Dee was heavily influenced by the Kabbalah (or Cabala), a system of interpreting the scriptures that finds significance in every letter and number. As mentioned earlier, Nostradamus also studied this mystical system. Dee was thought to believe in a pure form of the Kabbalah and to have used it for purposes of good. (While some people who refer to, or quote from, the Kabbalah may consider themselves clairvoyants or even witches, the Kabbalah itself should not be directly associated with the occult or witchcraft.)

Unlike some prophets, Dee was convinced that he did *not* have psychic abilities. He admitted that he was rarely able to see and hear spirits, although throughout his life he very much wanted to contact angels and other good spirits. This is why he felt he needed to enlist the help of others in contacting the spirit world. Unfortunately, this desire proved to be his undoing.

His Life and Times

Dee was born in London in 1527, the son of a minor palace official of King Henry VIII's court. In France, Nostradamus was in the last years of his productive life, and his legacy of prophecy was already influencing the spiritualism that Dee would advance. Both queens who ruled England during Dee's adult life were daughters of Henry VIII: Mary I (1516–1558), whose mother was Catherine of Aragon (1485–1536); and Elizabeth I (1533–1603), his daughter by Anne Boleyn (1505–1536).

Dee's brilliance was discovered early. He entered Cambridge when he was only fifteen years old and studied under the innovative Gerardus Mercator (1512–1594), a Flemish map maker known as the "father of modern geography," whom Dee greatly admired. By passing on his vast store of geographical knowledge to Dee, Mercator ensured Dee's later influence on nearly all the New World explorers of his day under the reign of Queen Elizabeth.

While at Cambridge, Dee was an avid student who vowed to spend only four hours a day sleeping, two hours eating, and the rest of the time studying. Judging from his achievements, he probably kept that adolescent resolution.

Stage magic

While still in school, Dee found time to pursue one hobby: theater special effects. Commentaries on Dee's life rarely mention his work in the theater. Even profiles of him as a prophet usually ignore his contributions to the arts of stage design and effects. The professional skeptic James Randi states that, despite this respected image, Dee "was never reluctant to mix a little attractive claptrap in with his otherwise valuable teachings." He seemed to know the importance of perception; he was, after all, a pioneer in theatrical special effects in an age when the audience believed them to be real and the result of magic.

Dee's own mechanical stage marvels aroused "general wonderment and sinister rumors" that he was possessed. Applying what he learned about theater from his younger days in Paris, Dee constructed amazing stage effects, such as those that made "supernatural spirits" appear and disappear. For a Greek drama being produced by his university, he built an intricate prop, a giant beetle to transport the hero. The audience was amazed when the beetle suddenly flew into the air, lifting the actor to the ceiling. Some were, in fact, more fearful than delighted, reportedly shouting out "Sorcerer!" This act sealed Dee's reputation as a conjurer and a magician, and his influence grew. Later, during his travels, Dee saw other "strange self-moving" devices used in theater productions. He knew they were operated by machinery, yet they still filled him with awe.

Dee was reportedly so well-respected at Cambridge that he was named a junior faculty member at just-founded Trinity College. Hungry for a broader education, however, Dee dropped out of post-graduate studies when he was about twenty to study math and other subjects at the University of Louvain, a great center of new learning. There, Dee studied the teachings of former Louvain resident Cornelius Agrippa, who taught that magic was a legitimate means of acquiring "greater knowledge of God and Nature." As mentioned earlier, Agrippa's interest in the Kabbalah, which Dee came to share, was not unique, but the mysticism he brought to it was. Dee's fascination with Agrippa fostered his interest in alchemy and astrology, which deepened his knowledge of the occult.

Dee later traveled to Paris, where he gave a series of talks on the Greek mathematician Euclid. They were so successful that townspeople packed lecture halls and scaled walls to get a glimpse of him. The study of math and other classical sciences at the time was steeped in mystery, mostly because these fields had languished in Europe during the Middle Ages. In Dee's time, people who were learned in these subjects and could discuss them knowledgeably were nearly worshiped.

In Royal Company

While in Paris, Dee earned exceptional praise as an astrologer and was offered the position of Royal Mathematician to the French court. However, he refused the position and returned to England.

Henry VIII's successor was his only son, Edward VI (1535–1553), who reigned briefly from 1547 to 1553. Edward began his rule when he was just ten years old, and Dee dedicated one of his early books to the young king. Edward's tutor, Sir John Cheke, had befriended Dee at Cambridge, and he encouraged the king to give Dee a yearly pension. Unfortunately, that financial security, which afforded Dee time to write treatises on the tides and stars, ended when the king died six years later.

Before the king's death, however, Cheke introduced Dee to Geronimo Cardano, or Jerome Cardan (1501–1576), an esteemed physician who had been summoned to the court to treat Edward while he was ailing. Cardano's relationship with Dee seems to have been a brief yet powerful one. Cardano, thought to be a witch by some, claimed to be guided in everything he did by a spirit, and to have out-of-body experiences and prophetic dreams. He published a paper in which he noted that it should be possible to change base metals into silver and gold, a practice known as alchemy. Cardano also told fortunes, but not always accurately. His prediction that Edward would have a critical illness at the age of fifty-five years, three months, and seventeen days was far off the king's actual death at age sixteen. Still, Dee appeared to have been impressed enough with the physician to adopt many of his beliefs. These included the desire to be guided by angels and to find something known as the philosopher's stone, which was believed to be the key to unlocking the secret of alchemy.

Guide to the queen

Following the death of Edward VI, Mary I ruled from 1553–1558. She became known as "Bloody Mary" because her reign was marked by the persecution and deaths of many Protestants. During Mary's reign, her half-sister Elizabeth was made a political prisoner because of religious strife between Catholics and Protestants. While imprisoned, Elizabeth sent for Dee to prepare her astrological chart. He made the mistake of comparing her chart to Queen Mary's, and his horoscopes were overheard by one of Elizabeth's attendants, a spy for Mary. This attendant spread the story that Dee had predicted both a long life for Elizabeth and Mary's death by magical means. Accused of plotting to kill Mary I, Dee was arrested, tried in what was known as the Star Chamber, and briefly imprisoned. Luckily, he was acquitted, avoiding the execution that was all-too-common in that day.

After that, Dee was frequently suspected, as was Nostradamus years before, of trying to take action to fulfill his own prophecies. However, as he came to be a favorite of Queen Elizabeth, he was largely protected from accusations of witchcraft. Not so lucky was the prophet Kenneth Mackenzie of Scotland, profiled in the next chapter, whose prediction of misfortune for the ruling family there earned him a cruel execution. Nostradamus aroused similar fears when he predicted Henry II's death.

Clairvoyant, Magician, or Spy?

Dee was called "the last royal magician" because he became Queen Elizabeth's astrologer. He provided many important services, including predicting the best day for her coronation in 1558. Dee also designed innovative hydrographical and geographical materials for the queen's newly claimed lands, and he encouraged Elizabeth to expand the British navy. He was consulted about astronomy and geography by the navigators to the New World, including Sebastian Cabot (1476–1557), Walter Raleigh (1554?–1618), Francis Drake (1540–1596), and Martin Frobisher (1535–1594). According to James Randi, "By direct order of Elizabeth, none of her appointed seafarers left port before Dee had contributed his valuable cartographic and navigational skills to their efforts."

Dee's influence on Elizabeth in international matters led to one of the more interesting speculations that has survived through the years: that Dee was spying for the queen. One biographer, Richard Deacon, theorized that he might have been one of the early members of the English Secret Service, responsible for collecting and passing on confidential information gathered during his extensive travels. During Dee's years with partner Edward Kelley, a scoundrel described later in this chapter, the two devised a bizarre language called Enochian, which some believed was also used to convey top secret information. This may not be as far-fetched as it seems. In *Visionaries and Seers* (Prism Press, 1988), Charles Nelson Gattey writes:

> Elizabeth's letters to him [Dee] usually began "My noble Intelligencer" or "My Ubiquitous Eyes," while he cryptically signed his communications to her with two circles (representing his eyes) followed by a figure seven with its top part extending backward over the circles.

In numerology, seven is the number of mystery. In this century, of course, Ian Fleming was to give his character James Bond the same code signature of "OO7."

A Man of Science

By the mid-sixteenth century, the Julian calendar was obsolete because it no longer corresponded to the seasons. Dee used his mathematical brilliance to design an adaptation of a new calendar for England, but it was refused. In 1582 a scientific group assembled by Pope Gregory XIII devised a new calendar, now called the Gregorian calendar, which is in common use today.

As did Nostradamus several years earlier, Dee shared the astronomer Copernicus's (1473–1543) belief in the revolutionary notion that the earth revolved around the sun. Commentators have claimed that Nostradamus, Dee, and other Copernicanists of their era were defying the church; however, the Holy Office at Rome did not issue an edict against followers of Copernicus until 1616, several years after the deaths of Nostradamus and Dee.

The popular culture of the day, following the example of royalty, was greatly influenced by astrology, prophecy, and predictions, even though church authorities condemned all but their own superstitions. The public appeared both to embrace and fear prophesies. While Dee was respected by explorers for his geographic and cartographic knowledge, and by Elizabeth for his visions, others appeared to condemn him for these same talents.

Unlocking the Unconscious through "Scrying"

Early in his formal education Dee mastered optics, which may explain how in 1581 he became fascinated with glass, crystal, and mirrors for use in his initial scrying experiences. Scrying is a method of producing visions by concentrating on a reflective surface, such as a bowl of water or a glass or crystal object, so that the practitioner can discover what is hidden in his or her own unconscious mind. This concentration also makes the scryer more receptive to telepathic messages and can help bring to the surface what is latent or unknown.

Scryers have reported seeing visions actually behind or within their crystals. These accounts support the popular image of the crystal-ball gazer as merely a passive receiver of an image seen within the crystal. Yet, the experience of scrying requires that the user be actively involved.

As mentioned earlier, Dee himself was not able to achieve communication with the spirit world; he needed someone else to do that for him. This is why he employed partners who claimed they were successful at this art. Dee performed important functions, however, as the facilitator, translator, and recorder of otherworldly encounters.

Dee considered his first scrying experience an important event, and duly recorded it in his diary.

Here is Dee's diary entry [rendered in modern English] about his first scrying experience with his most famous and long-lasting partner, Edward Kelley:

> He [Kelley] settled himself to the Action, and on his knees at my desk, setting the stone before him, fell to prayer and entreaty, etc. In the mean space, I in my Oratory did pray and make motion to God and his good creatures for the furthering of this Action. And within one quarter of an hour (or less) he had sight of one in the stone.

To give a sample of the actual language of Dee's day, here is a direct quotation from Dee's diary. The letters "E. K." refer to Edward Kelley.

Now the fire shot oute of E. K., his eyes, into the stone agayne. And by and by he understode nothing of all, neyther could read any thing, nor remember what he had sayde. . . at his side appeared three or fowr spirituall creatures like laboring men, having spades in theyr hands and theyr haires hanging about theyr eares. . . . Still they cam gaping or gryning at him. Then I axed him where they were, and he poynted to the place, and in the name of Jesus com-maunded those Baggagis to avoyde, and smitt a cross stroke at them, and resently they avoyded. . . .

In Search of Angels

One of the rare psychic experiences that Dee records in his diary involves seeing Uriel, the angel of light mentioned in the Kabbalah. Dee writes that he saw Uriel floating in the air outside his window. The spirit was holding a rose-colored crystal, which it gave to Dee. He also claimed that another apparition, the archangel Michael, told him how to use it. This crystal is now in the British Museum, along with anoth-er of Dee's favorite possessions, an Aztec "magic glass." This was a mirror seven inches in diameter obtained in Mexico between 1518 and 1521 by the Spanish conquistador Hernán Cortés (1485–1547). A wand and some of Dee's magic for-mula books are also part of the British Museum collection.

Dee also recorded that at one point he saw the archangel Gabriel, who promised to make him wise and wealthy. Randi states, "It was in response to this seemingly uncelestial promise that Dee abandoned his really important work to pursue psychic matters. The bargain was not kept by Gabriel though respected by Dee."

Dee's conversations with angels are taken very seriously by scholars of the Renaissance.

An Unsuitable Match

Hoping to find an assistant who would help him encounter the spirit world, Dee took on a series of partners, each of whom claimed to have a power Dee felt he lacked. He also hoped these individuals could help him find the legendary "philosopher's stone." Dee's goals illustrate how even the most brilliant people of his era were highly influenced by myths and superstitions inherited from less enlightened ages.

Dee's first partner was a young man named Barnabas Saul, who stayed with him only briefly. Then in 1583 he linked up with the notorious Edward Kelley for several years. Finally Dee associated with a Bartholomew Hickman, who claimed he had visitations with the angel Raphael.

Edward Kelley

Dee was a highly respected, almost saintly scholar, while Edward Kelley (1555–1595) was anything but. The rocky adventures of Kelley could fill several gothic novels. His biographers sometimes refer to him as disturbed but brilliant. He was an apothecary apprentice turned psychic, mystic, thief, prisoner, and charlatan. He was also an attempted wife swapper and was once arrested for necromancy—fortune-telling through contact with the dead. Some sources say that Kelley's cropped ears were a legal punishment for that act, while others say he received this punishment for forgery. Dee does not mention necromancy in his diaries and was most likely not associated with Kelley in this practice.

Kelley was believed by some to be possessed by evil spirits. In any case, it seems that he and Dee quarreled continually. But Kelley had a powerful trump card: He claimed he could communicate with angels. In fact, this was the main reason Dee associated with such a dubious character. Kelley also said that he knew the alchemical secret of transmuting base metal into gold—a lie that led to years of strife between the two men. If Kelley had been able to perform such a miracle, which obviously he couldn't, they would both have been very rich.

The Magical Language of Enochian

As mentioned earlier, in 1582, during eighteen of their scrying sessions, Kelley and Dee "received" a mystical, "angelic" language they called Enochian. Dee claimed that this language was spelled out to him backwards, so as not to overpower him and others with its dangerous force. The odd, backwards, and mirrored script that Leonardo used is sometimes considered mystical for similar reasons, even though Leonardo was usually writing about very secular topics.

Dee recorded Kelley's clairvoyant messages. Dee, or the two together, developed a language, rites, and rituals, which made up the Enochian system of magic. It was a real language, with its own grammar and syntax. In fact, a dictionary of the Enochian language has been published.

According to *The Encyclopedia of Witches and Witchcraft*, "Some maintain that Kelley, who had a reputation for fraud, invented Enochian and that it was a secret code that he and Dee used in espionage activities for Queen Elizabeth I. If Kelley did this, he was a master of magic, cryptography, astrology and mathematics, the elements of which are all embodied in the language."

Enochian became one of three magical systems taught by the Hermetic Order of the Golden Dawn, an influential occult society of the late nineteenth and the early twentieth centuries. Member Aleister Crowley (1875–1947), the notorious English poet, occultist, and magician, stated in his autobiography that the Nineteen Keys of the Enochian ritual that Dee organized actually could be used to communicate with angels and spirits. He published a comprehensive commentary on the keys in his book, *The Vision and the Voice* (1911).

Travels with Kelley

During their stormy relationship, Dee and Kelley traveled widely together, especially between Cracow and Prague, trying to raise money. They visited Holy Roman Emperor Rudolf II (1552–1612) in Prague because Rudolf, himself a dabbler in alchemy, was a likely patron.

Dee and Kelley also visited Poland, where they tried to convince King Stephen that Kelley knew the secret of changing base metals into gold using the philosopher's stone. However, after receiving many complaints about the "magic" practiced by Dee and Kelley, a papal edict officially expelled the two from the country.

Domestic Troubles

Dee's first wife died in 1575 after they spent ten years together. His second wife lived just a year after they wed before dying of the plague. Dee then fathered eight children with his third and last wife.

Meanwhile, Kelley was apparently frustrated in his marriage. He told Dee that a nine-year-old girl had appeared to him naked during a scrying session and ordered the two to swap wives. (Dee's third wife was reportedly very beautiful.) Dee prayed over the directive, apparently concluding that swapping wives was God's will. However, Dee's wife hated Kelley and was reportedly hysterical about the proposed arrangement. Nonetheless, she was resigned to her husband's reluctant decision. Fortunately for her, the proposed swapping apparently never took place, however. And Kelley and

Dee dissolved their relationship shortly afterward, though, strangely enough, some biographers say it was Kelley who deserted Dee.

As was dramatically fitting for such an infamous character, Kelley was killed in 1595 while trying to escape from a Prague prison.

A World of the Occult at His Disposal

Even though scholarly books were expensive and comparatively rare in Dee's day, he owned the largest collection of books on the occult in England, numbering four thousand volumes. Some of these books also were works of art. The magnificent Pierpont Morgan Library in Manhattan now houses a portion of Dee's library. It was said that at the end of his life, Dee was so poor he had to sell off some of these prized books to survive. One famous book collector, Robert Bruce Cotton, was so convinced that Dee had buried some of these treasures he spent a great deal of time and money fruitlessly searching for them. Interestingly, Shakespeare's character Prospero, the protagonist of *The Tempest*, who was thought to be based on Dee, buried his books at the end of the play.

In 1563, Dee acquired a rare copy of *Stenographia*, a classic work on magical numbers and symbols written by a fifteenth-century Benedictine abbot named Johann Trimethius. Dee then produced his own book on these topics, *Monas Hieroglyphia*, one of seventy-nine manuscripts he is known to have written. Very few of these works, however, were published during his lifetime.

Unfortunately, many of Dee's prized possessions were stolen from his house by his enemies while he was serving as a medium for royalty and for the wealthy during his travels with Kelley.

A Quiet End

After Elizabeth died in 1603, James, the son of Mary, Queen of Scots, ascended the English throne. Dee had predicted the execution of James's mother, and the king took revenge on Dee by stripping him of all honors and income. However, Dee was appointed to a low-level position as warden of Manchester College for a year in 1603. He retired and lived in seclusion for the last four years of his life. In 1608, he died in poverty and obscurity, and is buried near his home in Mortlake.

John Dee's notable contributions to science, theater, and literature are unchallenged. However, his reputation as a prophet and seeker of mystical links to the spirit world, unfortunately, may have been forever tainted by his relationship with the notorious Edward Kelley.

KENNETH MACKENZIE

The Brahan Seer

Died in 1663

I see into the future and I read the doom of the race of my oppressor.

— Kenneth Mackenzie
"The Doom of Seaforth"

Scotland has long considered itself the traditional home of *taibhsears*, or seers. And the most celebrated of all the Highland Seers is Kenneth Mackenzie, or Coinneach Odhar (in Gaelic), who claimed that he received his mystical powers from a ghost.

The story goes like this: On one sixteenth-century night on the remote Scottish island of Lewis, a Highland woman, Mackenzie's mother, was grazing her cattle on the edge of a graveyard. Suddenly, the tombstones toppled to the ground, and the spirits of the departed flew out and away into the night. More curious than afraid, the woman waited patiently to see what would happen. One by one, the spirits came back to their graves, until only one grave remained vacant.

Following the superstition that ghosts could not reenter a grave marked with a distaff (a cane-like stick used in weaving), Mrs. Mackenzie stretched her own distaff over the open grave, hoping to block the last spirit's entrance so she could speak to it. Finally, the apparition, a young woman, returned and demanded that she be allowed to reenter her grave.

"Not until you tell me why you were so late in returning," Mrs. Mackenzie answered. Then the spirit told her a sad tale: She had been the daughter of a Norwegian king and had drowned while bathing. Her body had floated far away from home and was buried where it eventually washed up. She was late because she had the farthest to go to visit her homeland.

Satisfied, Mrs. Mackenzie removed her distaff. But before she reentered the grave, the spirit said she wanted to reward the woman for her bravery with a rare and valuable gift. The wraith told her to go look in a loch [lake], where she would find a blue stone to give to her son. This stone would give its possessor the gift of second sight. Mrs. Mackenzie found the stone, went home and gave it to her son, Kenneth, who was to become the most legendary seer in all of Scotland.

Another story about how Mackenzie came into his powers was this: While working as a farm hand he became rebellious toward the farmer's wife, who was mean and demanding. Tired of Mackenzie's disrespectful remarks, she plotted to murder him. One day, while he was out with the sheep, she brought him some food laced with poison. Finding him asleep, the woman lost her nerve, dropped the food beside him, and ran home. When he awoke, he found he was somehow prevented from moving by a smooth white stone that lay on his chest. He then had a sudden vision of the farmer's wife's evil plan, and to test it out, he fed the food to his collie, who died instantly. The stone, of course, was the mystical talisman that gave him his second sight.

Some believe that Mackenzie himself circulated these stories to lend drama to his fortune telling. Like many other prophets, he wasn't above embellishing a little to add mystery or allure to his visions. Still, it was his surprisingly accurate and detailed prophecies that solidified his reputation.

Biographers usually mention that Mackenzie was "the seventh son of a seventh son," a fact given much importance in some cultures. Such an individual is considered by these traditions to be clairvoyant, capable of casting spells and healing through touch. Even today in the United States, the Pennsylvania Dutch consider the seventh son of a seventh son born into a family of witches to be more powerful than other witches. And among the Gypsies, the seventh daughter of a seventh daughter also is believed to be able to predict the future accurately.

Mackenzie most likely established himself as an occult figure through scrying, the method of seeing the future reflected off a smooth surface practiced by many prophets, including Nostradamus and John Dee.

A Gloom-and-Doom Predictor

Mackenzie became known as one who foretold the "terrible and trivial." One day, while crossing a field in Drummossie, he was struck by a thought so powerful that he threw himself down and wailed. "This black moor shall be stained with the best blood in the Highlands," he reportedly cried. "Heads will be lopped off by the score, and no mercy will be shown ... on either side." He was standing on Culloden Moor, where a terrible massacre of the Scots occurred during a rebellion of 1746.

Believers in Mackenzie's predictions say that he foresaw these events (most relating to Scotland):

✧ Battle at Culloden
✧ Building of the Caledonia Canal

- ❖ Nuclear fallout and/or oil as "black rain"
- ❖ Introduction of sheep farming in the Highlands
- ❖ Subsequent depopulation of the area through mass emigration
- ❖ Return of the people to repossess their land
- ❖ Advent of railways
- ❖ Discovery of North Sea oil
- ❖ Ruin of the Mackenzie clan
- ❖ Financial disaster for the McNeils of Barra
- ❖ Takeover of the land by "strange merchant proprietors"
- ❖ Doom of the Seaforth family line

Here are a few in more detail.

The cow in the tower

According to historian Magnus Linklater, Mackenzie once told a large crowd that the Mackenzies of Fairburn would face ruin when a cow climbed the steps of a castle tower and gave birth to a calf in the topmost chamber. People laughed when they heard this, because the tower was occupied by a rich and powerful chieftain. In the 1800s, however, the castle fell into disrepair, and a nearby farmer began using the tower to store hay. One day, a pregnant cow found the door open, went in, and climbed up the stairs following the trail of hay. In her condition she was too big to get back down, so the farmer let her stay until she gave birth. Locals who remembered Mackenzie's prediction reported it to the newspapers.

"That unlikely event duly took place in 1851, and became so celebrated that special transport had to be laid on from Inverness for curious sightseers to witness the result. The luckless family fulfilled the prediction by dying out," wrote Linklater.

Financial disaster for the McNeils

Concerning the curse on the McNeils of Barra, Linklater reports that Mackenzie said that financial disaster would befall them when a "big-thumbed Sheriff Officer and a blind man of twenty-four fingers were found together on the island." Again, as unlikely as that seemed, popular Scottish lore says that in 1838 a blind, wandering panhandler with six fingers on each hand and six toes on each foot crossed over to Barra on the same boat as a sheriff. The sheriff was on his way to the McNeils to serve them an eviction notice. The McNeils declared bankruptcy soon afterward.

Future Shocks

A bridge to war

Mackenzie also predicted that the day more than four bridges were built across the River Ness, a frightful disaster would involve the nations of the world. Even with the well-known curse in mind, in August 1939 a temporary fifth bridge was constructed across the river. For a few days, it seemed that finally a Mackenzie curse was not going to come true. However, on September 1, Hitler invaded Poland, after which all the major world powers became involved in World War II. To those who swear by the Mackenzie prophecies, this was further proof of Mackenzie's long-range vision.

A hornless cow

Another puzzling prediction has taken on ominous meaning in hindsight. Mackenzie had foreseen a "dun horn-less cow" that would appear in a river near Gairloch, and bellow so loudly that it would cause the six chimneys of Gairloch House to fall. After this, the whole country would become desolate, and deer and other animals would die from "horrid black rain." Today, believers say that Mackenzie was describing atomic submarines, based in the Holy Loch a short distance from where Mackenzie saw the hornless cow. They could certainly cause a violent explosion, or "bellow."

The black rain is interpreted as radiation fallout. While these ideas can be chalked up to leaps of the imagination, it is nonetheless interesting to note that while Mackenzie was alive Gairloch House had no chimneys. Today, it has six.

A sinking feeling

Journalist Alan Crow quoted folklore expert Kenny Dan Smith on Mackenzie's accuracy: "So many things he has said have come true, but not always in the way first imagined." As with the quatrains of Nostradamus, it doesn't pay to take a Mackenzie prophecy too literally. This is especially true when there is no written material to support it. For instance, rumors persist that Mackenzie had predicted that "the Isle of Lewis will sink with no survivors." Naturally, local residents thought first of the actual island. However, in 1995 a ferryboat named *Isle of Lewis* was launched by Princess Alexandra at Port Glasgow. Many then assumed that this boat would be the object of the prediction. A 1995 article published in London's *Daily Mail* voiced concern about Mackenzie's prophecy: "A new ferry to the Western Isles is to keep its name, the *Isle of Lewis*, although many islanders have vowed not to sail on it because of a supposed sixteenth-century prophecy." To date, the ship is still afloat.

On the island itself, uncertainty lingers, despite the ferryboat and the lack of evidence that such a prophecy was even made. "There are persistent island rumors that . . . Mackenzie . . . said the *Isle of Lewis* would sink with the loss of many lives," wrote Alan Crow in his 1996 *Scottish Daily Record* article, "Not Ferry Confident." The rumors are so strong that all books about Mackenzie were cleared from the local libraries. A government official regularly gives radio broadcasts so as to reassure the islanders. The radio announcement explains:

Not only is there no record of [the prophecy], but it certainly seems not to have even been handed down in the oral tradition through the generations like so many other of his predictions. If [Mackenzie] did say [the Isle of] Lewis will sink under the water, that is almost fulfilled each winter. Between November and this time of year, the rainfall is such that the island is almost constantly under water, anyway.

Sowing His Own Doom

During Mackenzie's own lifetime, these and other uncanny predictions drew the attention of wealthy families on the Scottish mainland, who sought his advice. Unlike Edgar Cayce, whom we will later see had to be convinced to charge any fee at all for foretelling, Mackenzie was reputed to be somewhat vain about his powers, and he charged high fees. He eventually became known as the "Warlock of the Glen" and, finally, "The Brahan Seer." Brahan Castle is the setting for Mackenzie's prophecy called the "Doom of Seaforth," for which he is most famous. Unfortunately for him, however, earning this nickname cost him his life.

Just as Mackenzie was comfortably enjoying fame and fortune, he was called into service by Isabella, wife of the third earl of Seaforth, who lived at Brahan Castle near Dingwall. Her husband was several months late in returning from a journey to Paris, and she wanted Mackenzie's help in locating him. The seer gazed into his stone and was said to have broken into a lewd smile. "He is well and merry," he told her. She wanted more details, which the seer at first refused to give her. When she persisted, however, he blurted out that he had seen the earl in a Parisian salon with his arms around another woman.

Jealous and enraged, the woman accused Mackenzie of trafficking with the Devil and swore he would suffer the worst punishment that could be inflicted for ruining the earl's good name. Records of the sixteenth-century Scottish parliament include an order to prosecute Mackenzie as a wizard, which Isabella probably instigated. Some say the earl rode up just as Mackenzie was about to be burned alive. Hearing the seer's prediction and knowing it was true, the guilty earl tried to get a stay of execution, but it was too late.

Before his death, Mackenzie unleashed his final prediction, which is now called "The Doom of Seaforth," viewed as a scathing curse on the family. This angered Isabella even more. Allegedly, as he was led to the stake, she jeered that he would never go to Heaven. He replied that while he would go there, she never would. Mackenzie told her that after his death a raven and a dove, flying in opposite directions, would meet over his ashes. If the raven landed first, she had spoken the truth. If the dove was the first to touch down, Mackenzie was in the right. Enraged, Isabella ordered an even crueler death for the prisoner than being set on fire (if that is possible). While there are different stories of exactly how this was done, one particularly gruesome version says that Mackenzie was placed head first into a barrel that was filled with burning tar and lined with sharp spikes. Some claim that just after his execution a raven and a dove did land on his remains. The dove, of course, was first.

A curse on your house!

The fulfillment of the Doom of Seaforth prophecy, down to the fine details, is one of the most amazing feats of clairvoyance to date. "I see into the future and I read the doom of the race of my oppressor," begins the curse. Mackenzie then spelled out the details of events he foresaw happening to the Seaforth family line. Here are a few excerpts, followed by what actually happened:

From the Doom of Seaforth (1663)

Predicted:	What Supposedly Occurred:
"I see a chief, the last of his house, both deaf and dumb. He will be the father of four sons, all of which he will follow to the tomb."	Some say the lord became deaf and mute in 1793 due to childhood scarlet fever, but regained his speech as an adult. Others say he was deaf as a child, but only lost his speech after the tragic early deaths of his four sons, which Mackenzie also predicted.
"There shall be four great lairds [landowners].... Gairloch, Chisholm, Grant and Raasay [Ramsay]—of whom one will be buck-toothed, another hare-lipped, another half-witted, and the fourth a stammerer. Chiefs distinguished by these personal marks shall be the allies and neighbors of the last Seaforth...."	The lords who became Seaforth's neighbors had all the characteristics that Mackenzie had mentioned. Gairloch was buck-toothed. Chisholm had a harelip. Grant was mentally slow. Macleod (of Raasay) had a speech impairment that caused him to stutter.
"The remnant of his possessions shall be inherited by a white-coifed [hooded] lassie from the East, and she is to kill her sister."	Mary Elizabeth Federica, heir to the estate, married an admiral named Hood and had to travel to India. After he died, she wore the traditional widow's white cap. She soon had to sell her lands to strangers. One day as she was driving a carriage with her sister as a passenger, the vehicle overturned, killing her sister.

According to Linklater, soon after World War II, "It was decided that this run of bad luck was too great to be continued. The castle was blown up, and each stone separated from the others. The present owner. . .waits to see whether he had done enough to placate the Brahan Seer and ensure the survival of the line."

Though his tale is shrouded with spirits, superstitions, and other unprovable details, few people have left more tenacious legends and oral traditions on a culture than did the Brahan Seer.

JULES VERNE
A Man Ahead of His Time
1828-1905

All that I imagined will remain below the truth, for a time will come when the creations of science will surpass those of the imagination.

— Jules Verne

While it may seem a stretch to call a novelist a prophet, the scope and accuracy of the works of Jules Verne are so amazing that he truly seemed able to see into the future. The brilliant French novelist is regarded as a pioneer, if not the father, of science fiction. His books are the most frequently translated of all French authors, attesting to his widespread popularity and the agelessness of his writings. And Verne not only shared his insights with readers down through the ages, he also enlightened his contemporaries and inspired explorations into the unknown. For example, Rear Admiral Richard Byrd said that it was Verne who "led" him on his polar expeditions. Other explorers, scientists, and inventors also have acknowledged their indebtedness to Verne's prophecies.

An Inventive Age

While Verne was a futurist, it was also obvious that he was very much a product of his time. When he was a teenager, his countrymen were making major progress in communications. In 1828, the blind musician Louis Braille invented the writing system named after him; in 1835, Louis Daguerre devised the form of photography known as daguerreotype; and in 1842, long before Verne published his first novel, his fellow Frenchman Henri Giffard invented the airship. By the time Verne had written *Five Weeks in a Balloon*, his first novella, inventors Alexander Graham Bell and Thomas Edison were only teenagers, and the Wright brothers had not yet been born. The world was in the early stages of a creative burst of energy that would last through the second half of the nineteenth century.

Against this backdrop of discovery, Verne began writing the fantastic, futuristic tales that were to inspire generations to come. His 1872 novel, *Around the World in Eighty Days*, secured his place in the world of literature and continues to be a popular classic. But it was his science fiction tales, such as *From the Earth to the Moon*, that would prove the most prophetic.

Early Life and Career

According to one account, when he was eight years old Verne decided to run away and travel around the world. Like most young wanderers he didn't get far, and in a moment of remorse told his mother that from now on, he'd do all his traveling in his imagination. Perhaps this is why he spent his life describing great adventures and voyages, whether on water, in the air, or in outer space.

Verne was the son of a magistrate, so it was natural that he first pursued a law degree. At one time he also worked as a stockbroker. Like many other prophets, however, Verne had some turning points early in his career that helped him realize his true calling. His grandson tells the story that in 1848, while working as a stockbroker in Paris, Verne saw a travel brochure describing a trip around the world. This sparked his wanderlust, and his creative imaginings began to take form through writing.

Around that time, Verne also became interested in the theater. He had some success writing operetta librettos and plays. As it was for Leonardo da Vinci and later, John Dee, the theater was an excellent outlet for expressing his fascination with the future.

Verne finally settled into writing, which allowed him to popularize science, mix humor with adventure, and share his ideas on new technology. He found his best creative voice in prophetic science fiction, which allowed his visions of the future to take flight.

Many of Verne's works first appeared as serials in a British publication for young boys edited by W. J. G. Kingston, who later came to be the most frequently used English translator of Verne's stories. The enthusiasm young people expressed over these serialized versions of Verne's stories contributed to the lasting (albeit false) impression that Verne was primarily a writer of juvenile fiction.

Influences

Some prophets are guided toward an exceptional life by a mentor in their childhood who recognizes their gift. The young Jeane Dixon was told by a soothsayer and then a priest that she would become an astrologer. Andrew Jackson Davis's clairvoyance was noticed by a neighbor who was a hypnotist. Young Evangeline Adams's insights were fostered by her family physician. The talents and career of Verne, too, were nurtured by such a mentor—publisher Jules Hetzel. The two men soon discovered that they had more in common than first names. They also shared an awareness of the public's hunger for fantastic adventure stories. Once Hetzel saw the enthusiasm of the young writer and heard his unprecedented ideas for stories, he became Verne's lifelong editor and publisher.

Another of Verne's major influences was not an individual, but a nation. Although he was certainly loyal to France, Verne was very enthusiastic about America. In twenty-three of his novels, American characters play an important role; and in many, the action takes place on American soil. Although Verne criticized American capitalism, Verne expert Jean Chesneaux points out that "In the world of the mid-nineteenth century it was the United States that came closest to the 'model for development' of which Verne dreamed."

Journey of the Mind

The success of his first work, *Five Weeks in a Balloon*, in 1863 prompted Verne to leave the legal profession and devote himself to writing. During the next two years in quick succession, he published *Journey to the Center of the Earth* and *From the Earth to the Moon*. Five years then passed before the publication of one of his best-loved works, *Twenty-Thousand Leagues Under the Sea*, in 1870. After that, he came to Paris with manuscripts of both *Around the World in Eighty Days* and *The Mysterious Island*. The former, published in 1873, was quite successful in its time and is still widely read.

Around the World in Eighty Days tells the adventures of London gentleman Phileas Fogg, who wagers a bet with fellow club members that he can journey around the world in the unbelievably quick period of eighty days. Through the course of the story he and his man-servant, Passepartout, travel by land, sea, and air to circle the globe, encountering dangers and obstacles of all kinds along the way.

To better appreciate Verne and capture the enthusiasm of his first readers, one must remember that a voyage around the world in *only* eighty days sounded like an impossibility in the nineteenth century, although now it may sound like a leisurely tour. The public later found that his idea was not only doable, but remarkably close to reality. In 1889, as a publicity stunt for his newspaper, Joseph Pulitzer challenged a rival New York City paper to a race around the world, and sent the indomitable American journalist Nellie Bly as his paper's representative. Bly circled the globe and returned to New York in the record time of seventy-two days, six hours, and eleven minutes. Her achievement is even more ironic and remarkable considering that she risked losing the record when she stopped over in France to visit Verne. Using a map of Phileas Fogg's imaginary journey, Verne showed Bly that he was marking each step of her well-publicized trip.

Amazingly, Verne's estimate of the time it would take to go around the world, which he had written about fifteen years earlier, was not much more than a week off Bly's actual time. (More than a century after *Around the World in Eighty Days* was published, the supersonic Concorde makes the around-the-world trip in one day, seven hours, twenty-seven minutes, and forty-nine seconds.)

Verne's Prophecies

Even prophecy skeptics acknowledge that many of Verne's forecasts were amazingly accurate. In his novels he described, often in detail, several of the scientific achievements of the twentieth century. Some of these were at least prototyped before Verne wrote about them, but they were not nearly as well-developed as they were in his fiction.

Before he would describe a fantastic device or event in his stories, Verne often would present real or plausible documentation to lay the scientific foundation for his "invention." Those who knew him said he had no pretensions of being a man of science, and he checked out his ideas with experts whenever possible. Verne was said to be meticulous in drafting his stories and novels, keeping remarkably neat drafts of manuscripts and going over each with a fine-toothed comb for errors. He reportedly required up to eight successive proofs of his novels and was said to have cost his editor quite a bit of money in hiring proofreaders.

Here are a few of the amazing technological advances he described in his works.

Missile launches

In *From the Earth to the Moon* (1865), Verne describes a blastoff to the moon taking place from a location in Florida. The fictional site is at nearly the same latitude as the Kennedy Space Center, where actual launches take place today.

In his biography of his grandfather, Jean-Jules Verne notes that the space vehicle described in the book "was the same weight and height as that used one hundred years later in the *Apollo 9* moon expedition, and it was launched from the same place—Florida."

In this biography, Jean-Jules Verne also includes the famous "splashdown" illustration as it appeared in *From the Earth to the Moon*. The caption states that the illustration "proved to be so prophetic when—one hundred years later (in 1968)—the American astronaut Frank Borman landed in the Pacific after the *Apollo 9* [sic] moon expedition—about two-and-a-half miles from the point mentioned in the novel."

(Actually, astronaut Borman was only on the *Apollo–Saturn 8* trip in 1968, the first lunar orbit.)

Jean-Jules adds that Borman wrote to him recalling that as a young boy he, like other space explorers, had been fascinated by Jules Verne's books. "In a very real sense he is one of the great pioneers of the space age," Borman said. Verne would have undoubtedly been thrilled to know of the fantastic voyage taken by a fan who read his works many years later.

Weightlessness

In *From the Earth to the Moon* (1865), Verne first wrote of weightlessness. We now know that this condition occurs when a spacecraft drifts in outer space. It also can be experienced in a space capsule orbiting the earth, or even in an elevator falling freely in a vacuum.

Space satellites

Round the Moon (1870), a sequel to *From the Earth to the Moon*, added some features to Verne's earlier idea of a satellite orbiting Earth. The first artificial satellite was launched in 1957 by the Soviets, an event foreseen by Jeane Dixon when she predicted years before Nikita Khrushchev came to power that a "silver ball" would be put into space while he was premier.

Animals in space

In *From the Earth to the Moon*, Verne foresaw the need to test the safety of space travel on animals before using humans. The first actual space flight with living animals is believed to have taken place in 1951, nearly a century after Verne's work. Four monkeys were launched eighty-five miles into space from White Sands, New Mexico. The project, "Operation Albert," was kept secret so as not to upset animal-rights activists.

Six years later, in 1957, the Russians launched *Sputnik II* with a dog (Laika) aboard. This was the first animal to orbit the earth. The dog was kept alive for ten days, proving that life could be sustained in space (that possibility had been accepted by Verne fans for some time). The satellite disintegrated in space six months later.

Guided missiles

Verne's unfinished work, *The Carsac Mission* (1914), describes remote-controlled missiles. Though rocket missiles, albeit not the guided variety, were used in 1806 by the British in a naval attack on Bologna, France, during the Napoleonic Wars, it was the Germans who developed the first surface-to-surface guided missile, the V1, in 1942.

Helicopters

The first sketch of a helicopter may have been drawn by Leonardo da Vinci in the fifteenth century, but the actual design of the first helicopter capable of lifting a person off the ground in vertical flight dates from 1905, one year before the Wright Brothers received their patent for a flying machine. Decades earlier, Verne portrayed an invention closely resembling a helicopter in a few of his stories, including *The Clipper of the Clouds* (1886).

Plastic

The helicopter-like vehicle Verne described in *Clipper of the Clouds* was made, in part, of a plastic substance. The first plastic, Parkesine, was produced by Alexander Parkesin in London in 1866, twenty years before Verne's book. However, Parkesin was one of many inventors who had made a significant discovery but did not realize its potential. He saw plastic only as "a beautiful substance for the Arts." Three years later, a similar thermoplastic was patented by John Wesley Hyatt of

Albany, New York, and was called celluloid. But apparently neither inventor envisioned anything so ambitious as building a flying machine with their materials.

Motion pictures

The debate about who invented the first motion pictures dates back to the 1930s, when the daughter of Louis Aimé Augustin Le Prince claimed that her father had projected moving figures onto a wall at the Institute for the Deaf in 1885.

Verne's descriptions were made shortly after Le Prince's experiments but were still ahead of the functional technology of the time. He imagined something like motion pictures in *The Castle of the Carpatheians* (1888), to name one example. In this story, a baron watches and listens to images and recordings of an opera singer.

Later on, also during Verne's lifetime, a sixteen-minute theater production was filmed, partly based on Verne's *A Trip To the Moon* (probably the first example of a science fiction movie). It was made in 1902 by the pioneering Georges Melies, known as "the Jules Verne of cinema." While both his movie and Verne's work had the astronauts fired from a large gun, Verne's characters orbited the moon, never landing. However, Melies had the spacemen actually land on the moon, and in that way also was inspired by H.G. Wells's *First Men in the Moon*.

Submarines

Sophisticated submarines like those Verne detailed in *Twenty Thousand Leagues Under the Sea* (1870) did not appear for many years after his book was published. Some of the features of Verne's submarine may never be realized, such as a luxurious salon with a 12,000-volume library, a museum of marine life, and an extensive art collection. However, many of the capabilities he foresaw have since been realized, including:

- ❖ self-propulsion
- ❖ capability of diving to the ocean floor
- ❖ maneuverability under water
- ❖ high speeds
- ❖ ability to launch sneak attacks on enemy surface ships
- ❖ wetsuits for divers

While each of these creations seemed revolutionary at the time, sometimes truth is even more surprising than fiction. Specifically, a one-man midget submarine actually existed and successfully attacked a British flagship as it lay at anchor in New York harbor in 1776, a century before Verne's *Twenty Thousand Leagues Under the Sea*. Moreover, the first submarine may date back even earlier. In 1624, Dutch physicist Cornelius Drebbel invented something resembling a submarine in London, two hundred years before Verne was born.

Verne was probably aware, too, that in 1797, the American inventor Robert Fulton (1765–1815) had begun trying to develop a practical submarine. In 1800, Fulton successfully demonstrated a submarine he called the *Nautilus*, a name Verne was to give the submarine in *Twenty Thousand Leagues*. Both are appropriately named after another ocean dweller of a very distant time—a subclass of mollusk that flourished 200 million years ago.

In any case, Verne's *Twenty Thousand Leagues* certainly popularized the idea of a powered submarine and explored its possible applications. This book also included his prediction of the discovery of the South Pole, which he accurately envisioned would be almost entirely submerged under water. His other predictions in the novel included several ways to apply electrical power:

- ❖ clocks
- ❖ heating coils
- ❖ cooking stoves

- ❖ lights
- ❖ searchlights
- ❖ generators for large engines

Predictions in Verne's *Twenty Thousand Leagues Under the Sea* that have not yet come true include the following:

- ❖ The ruins of Atlantis will be discovered.
- ❖ The ocean will become the source of all food.
- ❖ The following will be invented:
  - – underwater guns
  - – virtually invisible glass ammunition
  - – seaweed cigarettes (with nicotine)

Giant telescopes

In *From the Earth to the Moon*, Verne created a large telescope located very near where one of the two Hale Observatories was later built. Construction began in 1928 (sixty-three years after Verne's novel) on Palomar Mountain, northeast of San Diego, California. Work done at these locations helps to describe the size and shape of the universe, as well as the evolution of heavenly bodies. A large camera in one of the observatories was used in preparing a definitive atlas of most of the sky. Long before such scientific evidence, Verne, too, expressed curiosity about the vastness of the universe.

International telephone conference calls

Verne described what we would now recognize as international conference calls in his *The Day of an American Journalist in 2889* (1889), which he envisioned being made in the year 2000 between London, Vienna, Paris, St. Petersburg, and Peking. Perhaps even more interesting, another amazing "prophecy" he included in this story was a phono-telephoto device through which newspapers present moving pictures (with sound) of world events, at the moment they are taking place. This is very similar to live news coverage via Internet newspapers, just now in development at the time of this book's publication.

Chemical warfare

A world on the verge of a devastating war was the subject of Verne's *The Begum's Fortune* (1879). Here, Verne describes war-related inventions, including "carbonic acid gas," a deadly weapon at the disposal of a sinister German named Schultz. Verne's Schultz was evil and saw his countrymen as a master race designed to rule the world. He is uncannily similar to the same evil individual called "Hister" by Nostradamus more than three centuries earlier.

H. G. Wells, strangely enough, is sometimes credited with predicting gas warfare in his *Things to Come* (1933). However, the first poison gas attack was launched by the Germans against the French in 1915. Many thousands of soldiers on both sides in World War I became victims of this form of warfare, including Corporal Adolf Hitler. Not surprisingly, in light of this development, the first Civil Defense units, not unlike those described in *The Begum's Fortune*, were established in 1915 in Britain.

Energy accumulators

In *The Day of an American Journalist in 2889*, Verne describes transformers that would store and recycle energy from waterfalls, rivers, wind, the sun, and the earth. Except for his vision that the heat of summer would somehow be stored for use in winter months, the other natural sources of energy were at various stages of evolution in his day. Again, it was his imaginative application of these inventions that reveals his foresight.

The first electric power station was a hydroelectrical plant, the Central Power Station at Godalming, in Surrey, England, installed in 1881. It was in operation only until 1884. The first electrical power station began operating in London shortly after the hydro plant, in 1882, seven years before Verne's story about the year 2889.

Verne's countryman and contemporary, Augustin Mouchot, built solar-powered steam engines, one of which operated a printing press in Paris in 1882. In America, Charles Greely Abbot earned the title "father of modern solar energy" by dedicating his life to experiments on the many practical applications of solar energy.

Windmills were used in America as a source of energy from the 1890s, although they were not yet the major contributor to energy conservation that Verne had envisioned.

Motor caravans

The characters in Verne's *The Steam House* (1880) travel across India in a luxury motor caravan. According to *The Book of Firsts*, it was not until 1901 that the first actual motor caravan was built in Paris. The owner, Dr. E. E. Lehwess of Germany, set out from London in 1902 to become the first man to drive around the world. The caravan was abandoned in a snowdrift in Gorki, Russia, only one-fifth of the way to its destination. Verne, on the other hand, wisely situated his trek in a warm climate.

Verne obviously shared Leonardo da Vinci's fascination with how people would get around in the future. In *The Day of an American Journalist* he envisioned cars, buses, and trains traveling through the air. Also, he imagined trans-Atlantic submarine tubes that would move people from Paris to America. With his typical love of detail, Verne stated that people would travel through the submerged tube from Paris to New York (Centropolis) not in five hours, but in 295 minutes.

Other inventions anticipated by Verne include:

- ✧ atomic energy capable of destroying an entire city
- ✧ seaplanes for travel under, on, and above water
- ✧ piped-in music
- ✧ videophone ("telephote")
- ✧ interplanetary communication
- ✧ global climate control
- ✧ food piped directly into homes
- ✧ robotic bathrooms
- ✧ advertising projected onto clouds
- ✧ energy accumulators with unlimited power
- ✧ cryogenics
- ✧ computers ("totalizers")

Other Voices

Many other writers have written prophetic fiction about space flights and journeys into other worlds. Beginning with Lucian of Samosata (c. 120–200), the more familiar authors of such journeys include Savinien Cyrano de Bergerac (1619–1655), Daniel Defoe (1660–1731), and Edgar Allan Poe (1809–1849). Poe was likewise interested, especially near the end of his life, in the journey to inner space and the psychic aspects of prophecy.

Famous writers since Verne who have been especially interested in the journey to other worlds, especially to Mars, include H. G. Wells (1866–1946) and the prolific Edgar Rice Burroughs (1875–1950). More recent science fiction writers who have successfully predicted space flight to Mars include Brian Wilson Aldiss (b. 1925) in *Who Can Replace a Man?* (1965) and David Guy Compton (b. 1930) in *Farewell, Earth's Bliss* (1966).

As mentioned earlier in this chapter, some inventions envisioned by Verne or others were credited to H. G. Wells. It's interesting to note that Wells, in comparing himself to Verne, had this to say in the preface to *Seven Famous Novels* (1934):

> These tales [of mine] have been compared with the work of Jules Verne and there was a disposition on the part of literary journalists at one time to call me the English Jules Verne. As a matter of fact there is no literary resemblance whatever between the anticipatory inventions of the great Frenchman and these fantasies. His work dealt almost always with actual possibilities of invention and discovery, and he made some remarkable forecasts. The interest he invoked was a practical one; he wrote and believed and told that this or that thinking could be done, which was not at that time done. He helped his reader to imagine it done and to realize what fun, excitement, or mischief would ensue. Many of his inventions have "come true." But these stories of mine collected here do not pretend to deal with possible things; they are exercises of the imagination in a quite different field. . . . They are all fantasies; they do not aim to project a serious possibility; they aim indeed only at the same amount of conviction as one gets in a good gripping dream.

Verne's Telling Details

Unlike the vague and ambiguous statements made by many prophets, from Nostradamus to Dixon, Verne's writing talents allowed him to pen descriptions that often were very specific and full of fanciful details. For example, in *A Trip To the Moon* (1865), he anticipated several details of the interiors of actual spacecraft of a century later:

The upper part of the walls were lined with thick padding of leather, fastened upon springs of the best steel. . . . The entrance into this metallic tower was by a narrow aperture contrived in the walls of the cone. This was hermetically closed by a plate of aluminum, fastened internally by powerful screw-pressure. The travelers could therefore quit their prison at pleasure, as soon as they should reach the moon.

Interestingly, Verne's fictional spacecraft in *A Trip to the Moon* was named *Columbiad*, eerily close to the name of the actual 1981 spacecraft, *Columbia*.

Growing Popularity

Verne was awarded the prestigious Legion of Honor medal in 1892, a year during which a few of the many contraptions he had envisioned were actually invented. The first automatic telephone switchboard was introduced that year. Rudolf Diesel patented his internal-combustion engine, and wireless telegraphy was being developed. As the world saw several of Verne's fantastic devices actually come to life, he experienced enormous popularity and was awarded many other honors. To illustrate Verne's popularity in his own day, author Peter Haining mentions that a number of people actually believed that Verne had been to the moon and back, and would ask if they could accompany him on his next voyage! Today there are 224 editions of various Verne works in twenty-three countries. Even in his own lifetime, 1.6 million copies of his books were sold in French alone, before their translation into other languages.

Verne's Lasting Appeal

An 1863 Verne essay called *Paris in the Twentieth Century*, a critical description of the future, was discovered and translated for the first time in early 1995, more than a century after it was written. The essay takes place in 1960, in a world where business has replaced art and poetry. Anticipating today's ongoing debate in the United States over art and obscenity, Verne's essay features an artist named Courbet who urinates onto a wall and calls the result art. Paris is polluted with auto exhaust fumes. On a positive note, he envisioned city streets lit by electric lights. France pays its citizens a dividend because there is a surplus of funds. And most significantly, there is no war.

Verne seemed to have a deep understanding of how progress could both benefit and destroy humankind. It was fitting that his last work, *The Eternal Adam* (c. 1905), was a warning against the misuse of science and technology. In the story, seven people face the task of rebuilding civilization after a global catastrophe.

Jules Verne was a man ahead of his time, who understood the power of science and technology with all their potential for both glory and devastation. His writings serve as windows to the future for the explorers and inventors in all of us.

ANDREW JACKSON DAVIS

The Poughkeepsie Seer

1826-1910

Any theory, hypothesis, philosophy, sect, creed, or institution that fears investigation, openly manifests its own error.

— Andrew Jackson Davis, *Memoranda* (1868)

American Andrew Jackson Davis was a clairvoyant with "vision" so sharp he claimed he could see through human bodies to diagnose illnesses and prescribe cures. While in a "magnetic sleep," he amazed people by speaking Hebrew and describing complex geographical and scientific facts—all subjects he had no knowledge of while awake. Davis was known to wander for hours in a trance, talking to the long-dead spirits of great thinkers. At the peak of his popularity, vendors sold statuettes of him. And he was thought to have inspired Edgar Allan Poe.

Despite many uncanny predictions and talents, however, Davis was haunted by critics who called him a plagiarist and a fraud; and eventually his star faded even during his own lifetime. Regardless of these naysayers, Davis truly seems to have been a medium through whom brilliant insights and healing flowed. His prophecies about the planets, architecture, and technical advances later proved to be dramatically accurate.

Davis was an important pioneer in the development of spiritualism. He made a convincing case that departed spirits could actually communicate through mediums. Before his death in 1910 he had penned more than twenty-five books on spiritualism and its relationship to religion and science.

The Poughkeepsie Seer

Davis was born in 1826, in Blooming Grove, New York. His childhood was difficult. His father, a sometime weaver and shoemaker, was a heavy drinker who barely scraped together a meager living. His mother was uneducated. The family lived in poverty, and Davis's formal education ended after about the fifth grade. Yet, before he was twenty, he was attracting learned professors and notable people who came to hear his lectures, which he would give while in a trance. Some of those who came did so not for the novelty of witnessing someone who could see into the future, but for the amazing knowledge that Davis was sharing.

An early calling

When he was twelve years old, while walking alone in a field, Davis "heard voices" and saw visions that urged him, among other things, to convince his father to move about thirty miles northeast of his hometown to Poughkeepsie, New York. (For a young boy, Davis must have had a great deal of influence over his parents.) Poughkeepsie was one of the cities on the Hudson that was growing rapidly during a time of expanding business and rail travel. The move to this larger city meant Davis was much more accessible to the intellectuals of his day, who were in a position to help spread his name and reputation.

Magnetic sleep

In 1843, when he was only a teenager, Davis attended a series of lectures on therapeutic hypnotism. When he tried it himself, however, he proved at first to be a poor subject who had difficulty entering the hypnotic state. Later, with the help of William Livingston, a local tailor and amateur hypnotist, he achieved what he called "magnetic sleep."

To Davis, a dreamy young man much absorbed in the power of the paranormal, this newfound ability opened up exciting possibilities. After learning the technique, he appeared to slip easily out of the flesh-and-blood world around him into one that seemed to swirl and pulse with incredible knowledge accessible only to the greatest thinkers of the past, present, and future.

At eighteen, Davis wandered from his home in a trance during which he said he met Galen, a famous Greek-born physician from the second century A.D., and Emanuel Swedenborg, a Swedish mystic who died in 1772. Galen's teachings served as a leading medical resource in Europe until the seventeenth century. One of his many discoveries was that the human pulse could be used as a diagnostic aid. He also was, along with Hippocrates, a pioneer in the understanding of what we now call human temperaments. Swedenborg will be described in greater detail later in this chapter. Though it is not known what transpired between them, the ideas of both apparitions had a profound influence on Davis. Medicine and mysticism became the two paths he followed most enthusiastically throughout his life.

Livingston discovered that Davis was able not only to hypnotize himself but also to give accurate diagnoses of diseases while "under." When he was in a trance, he said his patient's body became transparent to him; he could see where and what the sickness was. His practice of diagnosing and treating patients while in this state was strikingly similar to the methods used later by prophet Edgar Cayce (1877–1945), profiled later in this book.

Livingston saw the opportunity to promote Davis as a traveling faith healer. In New York City alone, Davis gave more than 150 lectures while in a trance. There were several other well-known traveling faith healers at that time. Metaphysical healing of the type performed by Davis also was practiced by his famous contemporary, Mary Baker Eddy (1821–1910). A major distinction between the two was Eddy's emphasis on the Judeo-Christian Scriptures. The most influential of her seventeen books is *Science and Health with Key to the Scriptures* (1875), which is still an official text for Christian Scientists.

In contrast to Eddy, Davis did not call upon organized religion or even emphasize Scripture in his healing. In fact, he doubted the Scriptures' absolute truth and described Christ as a moral reformer who was not in any sense divine. Davis's methods of healing related more to spiritualism than to religion.

Soon after demonstrating his unusual clairvoyant abilities, Davis was nicknamed "the Poughkeepsie Seer." Later, New York City newspapers would refer to him as "a medical clair-voyant," because he was able to prescribe cures simply by looking at a patient. Davis eventually lent credibility to his strange medical talent by earning a legitimate medical degree.

High-tech heaven

Hardly content with medicine alone, however, Davis also became a prolific writer, publishing books on a wide range of subjects. The most popular of his works was *Penetralia* (1856), which contained predictions about future inventions including air travel, gasoline, automobiles, and prefabricated buildings.

His vision of the new age, which he described as "a kind of material heaven," also included a phonetic spelling system and a typewriter that would help people convey their ideas as quickly as they occurred. Many of these technical advances had already been envisioned in the science fiction of Jules Verne and others, and some may have had prototypes in development. In formulating his vision of the future, however, Davis drew on extensive clairvoyant knowledge of several disciplines including science, math, and geography, none of which he had the slightest grasp of unless he was in a trance. He then communicated these thoughts to respectable scholars who witnessed his amazing transformations from an uneducated nobody to a genius whose mind appeared to be a window on the future.

The Influence of Swedenborg

Davis's manner of paranormal communication was not unlike that of the Swedish mystic, scientist, religious teacher, and engineer Emanuel Swedenborg (1688–1772). Author of many works on philosophy, humanism, the animal kingdom, the brain, and psychology, Swedenborg devoted his later years to the contemplation of spirituality. He believed that he alone had been chosen to receive God's true doctrines. Swedenborg developed a spiritualism outside the context of mainstream religion that spread throughout the world. Even though he had not intended to establish a new religious sect, his followers, often called Swedenborgians, organized themselves as the Church of the New Jerusalem. Swedenborgianism, which had a wide following throughout the nineteenth century, especially among intellectuals, included among its members the distinguished philosopher and psychologist William James (1842–1910), who influenced Evangeline Adams.

While some scholars refer to Andrew Jackson Davis as "the leading spiritist theoretician," this title probably belongs more appropriately to Swedenborg than to Davis.

Like Swedenborg, Davis's views on spirituality broke through the boundaries of the religious thought of his day. He wrote that everyone had an afterlife in a place called Summerland, where there was no real punishment. Davis said it would be "vastly more beautiful than the most beautiful landscape on earth."

Combining spiritualism with education, Davis founded a Lyceum movement featuring schools "in which teachers and students decided by voting . . . what was right and what was wrong. Instead of concentrating on reading, writing, and arithmetic, children discussed topics such as Summerland customs, death and dying, and 'the universal law of love.'" This dynamic movement was active and widespread during the first part of Davis's life, but it saw very little activity after the Civil War, as Davis entered his forties.

Contact with Apparitions

As noted earlier, Davis claimed to have seen at least two ghostly apparitions, Galen and Swedenborg, while in a trance. A person in a trance enters a state that falls between waking and sleeping, during which the mind is receptive to intuitions as well as to physical stimulation and other psychic phenomena. In 1850, Davis claimed to have visited a scene of violent poltergeist disturbances. (Poltergeists are spirits that typically manifest themselves by making noise or moving objects.) That year, Davis wrote his observations in *The Philosophy of Spiritual Intercourse*. Over the years his knowledge of apparitions and poltergeists grew, and he continued to write about them.

The Principles of Nature

In 1845, Davis began fifteen months of dictation that would eventually result in his most important book, *The Principles of Nature, Her Divine Revelations and a Voice to Mankind* (1847). This monumental task was performed in collaboration with a mesmerist, Dr. Lyon, and a scribe, the Reverend William Fishbough. The two assistants asserted that they made only grammatical corrections, leaving intact everything that Davis had said while he was in his magnetic sleep. This method is similar to that which Edgar Cayce later used with the help of his wife and an assistant.

In 1847, once his clairvoyant lectures were over, Davis described his trance experience in *Memoranda* (1868): "When delivering these lectures, I would receive impressions from the invisible world; and then, with my natural organs of speech, I would slowly, distinctly, and audibly deliver them to [Fishbough], in order that they should be accurately recorded. I would then return to the invisible world for another impression."

Credible Witnesses

Davis's amazing ability to lecture, prophesy, heal, and even speak in Hebrew was verified by learned individuals of his day. Highly respected witnesses to the Davis sessions included Davis's scribe, the Reverend Fishbough, and New York University professor of Hebrew, George Bush. Fishbough, who wrote letters to New York City newspapers about his experiences with Davis, said that Davis "displays, while in his superior state, a power of analysis and generalization perfectly unparalleled and absolutely overwhelming; though while in the normal state he is almost entirely *uneducated*. . . . The only rational explanation of this psychological phenomenon is that which Mr. Davis himself gives, viz.: that his mind, while in the abnormal state, receives the influx of the science understood in the spiritual spheres with which his mind associates."

Similarly, Bush wrote, "I can solemnly affirm that I have heard him correctly quote the Hebrew language in his lectures, and display a knowledge of geology which would have been astonishing in a person of his age, even if he had devoted years to the study, yet to neither of these departments has he ever devoted a year's application in his life." Davis's ability to spout Hebrew under hypnosis could be a form of *glossolalia*, the act of speaking or writing in a language other than the one(s) known by the speaker.

Bush also said that Davis "is continually giving forth in his lectures matter scientific, historical, theological, and philosophical, of a character so astonishing as to make entirely credible the narrative which I have related." He later said that "No prodigy of intellect of which the world has ever heard would be for a moment compared with him. Yet not a single volume on any of these subjects, if a page of a volume, has he ever read, nor, however intimate his friends may be with him, will one of them testify that during the last two years he had ever seen a book of science or history of literature in his hand."

Bush, a Swedenborg expert, also was impressed by Davis's incredible knowledge of Swedenborg's works even though the seer evidently had never read them before. One time, Bush asked Davis to help with some research he was doing on the Swedish spiritualist. The elderly professor had with him a manuscript he had written and that no one else had seen. In a strange turn of events, Davis requested that he be blindfolded so as not to see the manuscript, then he was put into a trance. In Davis's *Memoranda*, Bush recalls this session with Davis: "What is remarkable, although I had my

manuscripts [on Swedenborg] with me, from which I wished
to propose certain queries relative to the correctness of my
interpretation, I found I had no need to refer to it, as [Davis]
was evidently, from his replies, cognizant of its entire scope
from beginning to end, though all the time closely bandaged,
and unable to read a word by the outward eye. This will
appear incredible, *but it is strictly true.*"

The professor later risked his reputation by testifying to
the media and to others at his university that these events
really happened.

Critics ask why the bandage was necessary. Like many
seers before and after his time, Davis was surely aware of the
power of a little drama in convincing the public of one's special powers. Even the most sincere psychic evidently can see
the advantage of effective presentation.

Prophet or Plagiarist?

At times Davis's ability to recall, word-for-word, the writings
of others threatened to get him into trouble. His loyal friends,
Fishbough and Bush, however, were not among the doubters.
At one time Bush pointed out that he found strange coinci-
dences when sections of Davis's work, including a letter to
him, closely mirrored passages by Swedenborg written a
century earlier. Rather than charge Davis with plagiarism,
however, Bush was convinced that Davis's familiarity with
Swedenborg was based on the seer's trance-induced meeting
with the mystic years earlier.

Bush originally wrote to the *Tribune*, "My forthcoming
work [on Swedenborg] will contain a communication
addressed to me by Mr. Davis, written by him in his abnormal or ecstatic state, and made up of a series of quotations,
for the most part verbal, from a work of Swedenborg *which
he had never read!*" (The emphasis is Bush's.)

Whether to confirm his own confidence in Davis or to drum up publicity for his friend, in 1846 Bush offered one thousand dollars "to any person who will exhibit evidence that Mr. Davis has ever read or seen a copy of ... the Swedenborg ... works containing the ideas that [Davis] most frequently echoes in his Lectures. He has, moreover, in several instances quoted [Swedenborg's] works by their Latin titles, some of which are not known to be in existence in the original on this side of the Atlantic, and of which it is utterly incredible that he could previously have known anything at all."

Others were not so convinced of Davis's honesty, however. Raising suspicion about his integrity, scholars question not only his quoting of Swedenborg but also of an obscure author named Sunderland. They noticed that long passages in Davis's work *The Great Harmonia* (1852) correspond to an 1846 work on hypnosis by Sunderland called *Pathetism*. However, even one of Davis's main critics, Frank Podmore, believed that the Poughkeepsie Seer could not have intentionally plagiarized the Sunderland passages. Podmore wrote, "The explanation was to be sought in an extraordinary retentiveness of [Davis's] memory." Of course, similarities in the text could also be possible if Davis and Sunderland drew from the same psychic resources. Another explanation is that Davis was practicing a technique known as "remote viewing," a phenomenon that supposedly allows an individual to pick up experiences occurring great distances away or even in the distant past.

Predictions about Planets

Davis's trance-induced healing and linguistic powers were legendary while he was a young man. Yet his knowledge of astronomy while in an altered state was so incredible that he was one of a very select group to predict the existence of undiscovered planets. Davis's 1846 vision of an eighth planet occurred about the same time that the Englishman John Couch Adams (1819–1892) predicted the position of then-unknown planet Neptune. These predictions were made shortly before those of Frenchman Urbain Leverrier (1811–1877). However, the German scientist Johann Galle (1812–1910) was given credit for discovering the planet one day in 1846, after receiving Leverrier's predictions.

In 1846, Bush went on record in a letter to a newspaper saying that "young Davis's announcement of an eighth planet in our solar system, and even intimating that its elements had already been calculated [by Davis] months before anything was known of the fact in this country, must be admitted to be, in any mode of explanation, exceedingly remarkable, especially when it is considered that in his normal state he knows almost nothing of astronomy or of any other science." Davis's thoughts on other planets had been mentioned to numerous gentlemen "several months before the intelligence reached us of Leverrier's discovery," Bush noted.

Davis's fan, Fishbough, also firmly believed in the seer's knowledge of astronomy. "Mr. Davis has revealed the formation, constitution, geological development, inhabitants, and so forth, of all the other planets of our system," he wrote. (By "inhabitants" Fishbough is referring to Davis's belief in life on other planets, described later in this chapter.)

In Davis's work *The Principles of Nature*, he makes accurate statements about planets that had not yet been discovered by astronomers. Later, however, some commentators inaccurately claimed that Davis "discovered Neptune" and identified two additional planets.

Today's nonchalance about new planets may keep us from appreciating how dramatic Davis's predictions were some 150 years ago. His feat is noteworthy because despite his lack of formal education, Davis not only predicted the existence of a then-undiscovered planet, he accurately gauged its density, which agreed with astronomers' later calculations.

The ninth planet, Pluto, was discovered nearly a century later in 1930 by Clyde Tombaugh at the Lowell Observatory in Flagstaff, Arizona.

According to *Encyclopedia of the Occult* (1920), around the time of Davis's dictations, "A hypothetical planet was believed by astronomers to lie beyond Neptune and Uranus because neither planet followed the paths predicted by astronomers even when all known gravitational influences were considered. … Amid some controversy about the validity of the predictive process, Pluto was found nearly where it was predicted to be." It's difficult to tell, then, if Davis really had a jump on this ninth planet or was merely reacting to news he had heard.

As with most secular prophets, Davis's views did not always coincide with what we view as truth today (which doesn't always mean we are right, either). Although he predicted the existence of other planets, he spoke of only four *planetoids*. We now know there are hundreds. He also thought that our solar system and all the other stars revolved around an even greater center. Davis also believed that all but three of the nine planets held life. Compared to the level of development on Earth, Davis believed that the life was most advanced on Saturn, then on Jupiter and Mars, with the least development on Venus and Mercury. In 1848, Davis wrote: "And the world will hail with delight the ushering-in [of] that era when the interiors of men will be opened, and the spiritual communion will be established such as is now being enjoyed by the inhabitants of Mars, Jupiter, and Saturn."

A Prolific Writer

After dictating to a scribe during trances, Davis found that he could put himself into another state he called the "superior condition" and write about his experiences later. His books written after this revelation, then, were in his own hand rather than a scribe's. According to the *Encyclopedia of Occultism and Parapsychology* (1978), Davis "disclaimed dictation by the spirits and said that he could write them by some process of inner perception."

Davis began to teach and publish about mystical experiences. He would eventually write twenty-five books between 1845 and 1885. His works were mainly on spiritualism, some of which became best-sellers. *The Great Harmonia* (1852) went through forty editions.

A copy of the first edition of Davis's *The Herald of Progress* (1860) is in the New York City Public Library, as are *The Magic Staff*, his autobiography published in 1857, and the sixth edition (1881) of *Arabula: The Divine Guest, Containing a New Collection of Gospels*.

Poe and Davis

Davis's influence spread beyond spiritualism to touch the world of literature. The last published work of Edgar Allan Poe (1809–1849), best known for mysterious and macabre short stories such as "The Tell-Tale Heart" and "The Pit and the Pendulum," and poems like "The Raven," was *Eureka: A Prose Poem* (1848), published the year after Davis's *Principles of Nature*. Because of many similarities, scholars believe that Davis's work may have inspired Poe. This is highly possible: Poe expert Harold Beaver, in his study of Poe's works, notes that "large chunks" of Davis's *Principles of Nature* are quoted in Poe's *Eureka* (without credit going to Davis).

Poe attended several of Davis's trance lectures during which much of the technical material touched on in *Eureka* was addressed. Davis gave 157 lectures in 1845 alone, mostly about the advent of technology.

With the original edition of his spoof, *Mellonta Tauta*, Poe attached a farcical letter to his editor in which he says the work is "a translation, by my friend Martin Van Buren Mavis (sometimes called the 'Poughkeepsie Seer')," a clever pseudonym for Andrew Jackson Davis.

Davis on Poe

In 1846, shortly before writing *Eureka*, Poe visited Davis. Davis described his meeting with the mysterious writer:

> There is . . . something unnatural in his voice, and something dispossessing in his manners. He is, in spirit, a foreigner. My sympathies are strangely excited. There are conflicting breathings of commanding power in his mind. But as he walked in through the hall, and again when he left, at the conclusion of his call, I saw a perfect shadow of himself in the air in front of him, as though the sun was constantly shining behind and casting shadows before him, causing the singular appearance of one walking into a dark fog produced by himself.

A Humble End to an Amazing Life

Despite riding a crest of great popularity during certain periods of his life, Davis's later years were relatively uneventful. He ended his days in Boston, where he owned a small bookshop. He had acquired a medical degree and later wrote *Tale of a Physician* (1885). From his bookstore he prescribed herbal remedies to his patients. He died in 1910 at the age of eighty-four.

EVANGELINE ADAMS
Astrology's Champion
1868–1932

If we mean to have heroes, statesmen and philosophers, we should have learned women.

— Abigail Adams to son John Quincy Adams,
August 14, 1776

I n an age when people still believed in a "weaker sex," and when the suffrage movement was in its infancy, some of the most powerful individuals of the early 1900s came to rely on the prophecies of a fiercely independent woman named Evangeline Adams, who has been called "America's Nostradamus." An indirect descendant of Presidents John Adams and John Quincy Adams, Adams served clients including steel tycoon Charles Schwab, the popular actress Mary Pickford, the legendary operatic tenor Enrico Caruso, naturalist John Burroughs, financier J. Pierpont Morgan, the brilliant actor-director Charlie Chaplin, and King Edward VII, who reigned from 1901 to 1910. A half-century before the popularity of talk shows, Adams's reputation quickly spread within the social network of the rich and famous, as well as to the general population through her radio program, her newspaper column, and her newsletter, which reportedly had a readership of 100,000.

Astrology in the United States in the 1800s

According to astrologer Luke Dennis Broughton, at the time of Evangeline's birth in 1868 there were probably not more than twenty people in the United States who knew how to cast a horoscope. Yet Broughton eventually created a market for importing and distributing astrology books from Britain. Astrology publishing was productive in England at the time, although the actual practice of astrology was not yet accepted as legitimate by the courts. In America, Adams was soon to have a major influence on changing the general belief that astrology was akin to fortune-telling and illegal hoaxes.

By the time Adams won national attention at the turn of the century, there were thousands of amateur and professional astrologers in the country. Her influence was one of the main reasons for this amazing growth. Eloquent and influential, Evangeline Adams shared astrology's good news in lectures, columns, and radio shows. To modern times, popular astrologers—including the late Jeane Dixon, also profiled in this book—have followed in her pioneering footsteps.

Birth of an Astrologer

While her biographers usually mention correctly that she was "born into an influential New England family," some imply Adams was born in New England. Her actual birthplace was Jersey City, New Jersey.

Adams's father died when she was only fifteen months old. She then suffered a serious illness early in life, and her long recuperation provided an opportunity for the family physician to get to know her—and her unusual ideas. Noticing Adams's interest in the occult, the physician introduced her to his colleague J. Herbert Smith, a professor of Materia Medica at Boston University, who was known to integrate astrology into his practice as a diagnostician. After charting Evangeline's horoscope, Smith concluded that she could be a successful astrologer. Here, as was the case with Andrew Jackson Davis's hypnotist friend, an observant mentor played a large role in guiding her career. Smith, a student of Sanskrit and Eastern religions, taught Adams what he knew of astrology. He even came to hope that she could help him demonstrate that it was a science, as he believed it to be. Adams opened a local office in which she practiced until she moved to New York City.

Formation of a Prophetess

Adams attended a private school in Andover, Massachusetts. She was impressed by neighboring theological institutions, where she became involved with the occult circle gathered around the famous psychologist William James, founder of the Society for Psychical Research. There were at least three astrology-based religions in the United States as the twentieth century began: the Brotherhood of Light, the Esoteric Fraternity, and the Order of the Magi. As mentioned in the chapter on Andrew Jackson Davis, spiritualism is distinct from these astrology cults or religions. However, the popularity of both spiritualism and astrology was on the rise at the turn of the last century. This is a common phenomenon: Religions, cults, superstitions, and intense interest in the occult tend to flourish at both the beginnings and ends of centuries. This pattern is especially manifest at the end of millennia, as evidenced by the occurrences surrounding A.D. 1000 and by what we are seeing in connection with the year 2000.

William James had been influenced by Swedish mystic Emanuel Swedenborg (1688–1772), described in detail in the chapter on Andrew Jackson Davis (see page 79) and thus formed part of the chain of inspiration and intellectual development in mysticism that runs from the eighteenth century through the twentieth. A dynamic academic environment surrounded James in Boston when Adams was a student there. She undoubtedly was inspired by his lectures and his published works from this period.

Like Swedenborg a century earlier, and like her mentor James as well, Adams admired the mystical tradition of the British, dating back at least as far as psychic John Dee. Institutions having interest in the occult during Adams's day included the British College of Psychic Science (from 1920), later called the College of Psychic Studies, and the British Journal of Psychical Research (from 1926).

Adams also learned all she could from Smith, while simultaneously studying Vedanta under the distinguished Swami Vivekananda, a pioneer teacher of Hindu philosophy in the United States since 1893. He was the founder of the Ramakrishna Mission, the largest monastic order in India.

Coming into Her Own

Equipped with knowledge from her influential teachers, Adams evolved into the most popular astrologer of her day. She originated "Adams's Philosophy," which was her unique synthesis of occult theories from both Eastern and Western schools of thought.

During Adams's life it was rare for women to be in business for themselves. But Adams had a distinctly independent spirit, and she was not alone, as restless women of the time began to unite in suffrage organizations to fight for the right to vote. This practice spread gradually throughout the nation starting in the late 1800s. States taking the lead in this included Wyoming (in 1889), Colorado (in 1894), and Idaho (in 1896).

In 1899, Adams moved to New York City, where she saw that the atmosphere for change was not only in the stars for women in general, but specifically for herself. Even then New York was considered *the* city in which to meet and influence people.

Upon her arrival, Adams's choice of a particular New York City hotel would start a string of events that would change her life. In fact, that choice eventually led to circumstances that would allow her to share her insights with world leaders and millions of others.

The Breakthrough Prediction

It began on March 16, 1899, when, according to *The Book of Predictions*, "On her first night in New York, [Adams] settled into the Windsor Hotel . . . and provided proprietor Warren E. Lelane with a [n astrological] reading. Evangeline hesitated momentarily before telling him that she saw the next day— Friday, March 17—as a day of imminent danger for him."

Adams may have told the proprietor to make some significant change in his plans, such as to move with his family to another location. Unfortunately for him, he saw no need for extraordinary precautions after hearing Adams's prediction. (A similar disregard of an astrologer's warning also is described in the chapter on Jeane Dixon, whose warning of a presidential assassination was tragically ignored.)

Because the hotel was on Fifth Avenue, and March 17 was Saint Patrick's Day, many people participating in the famous annual parade were passing the building at the same time that a tremendous fire broke out within. At least one newspaper wrote that the blaze was caused by an unidentified man who had carelessly thrown a match onto a curtain.

The newspapers described how, at first, cries for help were drowned out by the noise of the parade. However, as several people leapt from hotel windows to their deaths, the hotel residents' screams finally were heard. At least fourteen people died in the fire. More than fifty others were injured.

Evangeline Adams is not listed in the papers as one of the hotel guests who escaped, yet obviously, she did. *The Book of Predictions* mentions that she "lost most of her possessions in the fire."

The Windsor Hotel fire of 1899 was significant in the history of astrology in the United States because Adams's dramatically fulfilled prediction about the proprietor drew widespread public attention.

After the fire, Adams took up residence in a Carnegie Hall studio. She was one of the earliest tenants of the historical hall, which opened in 1891. She would work and live there for the final thirty-three years of her life.

Legal Breakthrough for Astrology

Fifteen years after the Windsor Hotel fire, Adams was brought before a New York City court for violating a New York statute prohibiting the practice of "people who tend to tell fortunes." This was in 1914, when Adams was in her mid-forties. She was arrested as a "fortune-teller," but—always the opportunist—she decided to focus not on defending herself, but rather on presenting astrology as a science. She wanted to prove a long-overdue point, not only for herself, but for astrologers everywhere.

The trial delivered the kind of courtroom drama that would later be a staple of Hollywood movies. To test her, Judge John H. Frechi asked her to read the horoscope of an unidentified "person X." She was happy to comply. Adams proceeded to give startling details of the individual's present life and future. Rather than merely explaining the theory of her craft, she proved her point by interpreting the horoscope of none other than Frechi's son! The judge's natural familiarity with the details of his son's life, and Adams's undeniably accurate sketch of his character, impressed Frechi so much that he became a convert. His ruling in her favor meant that the practice of astrology was no longer prohibited in the state of New York. Part of his final statement is often quoted because it was a turning point in the history of astrology. "The defendant raises astrology to the dignity of an exact science," he said.

Inspired by her success in removing astrology from the category of illegal fortune-telling at home, Adams tried to have astrology legalized in Britain, as well.

Reaching the Masses

In 1930 and 1931, Adams gave astrological commentaries on the radio three times a week. This helped to generate some 300,000 letters written to her in one year alone, mostly from people seeking astrological advice. Even though she had a busy astrology practice, she also wrote a newspaper column and several popular books: *The Bowl of Heaven* (1926), *Astrology: Your Place in the Sun* (1928), and *Astrology for Everyone: What It Is and How It Works* (1931, 1941).

Successful Predictions

Death of Edward VII

For Adams, who cared greatly about the status of astrology in England, meeting and counseling Edward VII (1841–1910) must have been especially meaningful. After all, he was the eldest son of Queen Victoria (who reigned from 1837 to 1901) and grandson of George III (who reigned from 1760 to 1820). Adams is said to have correctly predicted the date of King Edward VII's death.

Abdication of Edward VIII

Even more remarkable, in one of her books Adams included an astrological chart of the bachelor Edward, then Prince of Wales, eldest son of George V. She saw in his chart that he would be interested in a married woman, even though public opinion would not accept the idea of a divorced woman becoming queen. Adams's commentary was written at least five years before Edward became king in 1936. Indeed, as she predicted, Edward fell in love with the married American, Wallis Warfield Simpson (1896–1986). This lady eventually divorced her second husband so that she could marry Edward. In order to marry Wallis, against the advice of the prime minister, Edward VIII abdicated in late 1936, saying he found it impossible to reign "without the help and support of the woman I love." Adams's prediction certainly proved true.

Bullish on the stock market

According to Manly P. Hall, founder of the Philosophical Research Society, Adams "was able to calculate the variations of the stock exchange so accurately that there was practically no difference to having read it in a ledger somewhere." But a critic, Gordon Thomas, in his book *The Day the Bubble Burst* (1980), gives the impression that Adams manipulated the information she gave her clients for her own personal profit.

In February 1929, Adams "predicted a dramatic upswing in stock prices for the coming months." The stock market, once considered a highly risky place to put your money, was now beginning to attract a whole new group of amateur financial speculators.

In May, the advice Adams gave to the 100,000 readers of her newsletter for the coming summer was, emphatically, to buy stocks.

On September 2, 1929, the hottest day of the year, a newspaper reporter asked Adams about the future of stock prices. "Her answer: the Dow Jones could climb to heaven. The very next day, September 3, the stock market hit its all-time high," the reporter wrote. Of course, it was soon to crash, and America fell headlong into the Great Depression.

Personal forecasts for J. P. Morgan

Adams also created monthly horoscopes for J. P. Morgan, advising him on the ups and downs of the stock market. Today, however, none of Adams's books or her correspondence with Morgan are to be found in the J. Pierpont Morgan Library in New York City.

Even so, a reporter once asked Morgan if it was true that millionaires consulted astrologers. He replied, "No. Billionaires do."

Enrico Caruso's death

Adams's reputation for accurate predictions drew the attention of stars from all galaxies. The great lyric tenor, Enrico Caruso, consulted her when he became seriously ill. During a performance at the Brooklyn Academy he began coughing blood, but continued the performance. In yet another show at the Metropolitan Opera, he performed even though he was gravely ill. Adams correctly predicted that Caruso would not die of this bout of illness. However, after the surgery that was expected to cure him, the tenor returned to Naples in 1921, where he was once again taken ill. This time Adams predicted that "He may die at any time." Caruso died two weeks later.

It is to her credit that with thousands of adoring fans and a world of experts from whom to draw advice, it was to Evangeline Adams that Caruso ultimately turned for guidance and counsel.

The victory of Warren G. Harding

It is sometimes said that Adams correctly predicted the landslide victory of dark-horse presidential candidate Warren G. Harding in the election of 1920. However, what Adams actually predicted—correctly—was that Herbert Hoover, at one point the leading Republican nominee, would not be nominated.

World War II

Adams's preference for bearing good news did not keep her from foretelling the ugliness of the future. It was always her hope that appropriate preparations would be made in time to avert an even worse outcome.

It is often said by the uninformed that astrologers simply tell people what they want to hear. However, if there was ever a time when a nation wanted to hear good news, it was during the Great Depression, which began in 1929. Yet, in 1931, Adams expressed an unpopular opinion by predicting that the United States would be at war in 1942. And, as the world now knows, the United States entered World War II in December of 1941.

Her own death

In her book *Astrology*, Louise MacNeice writes that Evangeline Adams predicted well in advance her own passing, which occurred on November 10, 1932. Also, a few days before she died, Adams "politely declined a twenty-one-night lecture tour that had been offered to her" for that autumn.

Six years after Evangeline's death in 1932, John Quincy Adams III was born. He was a very distant cousin of hers, but exceptional interest in the occult may run in the genes of the family: He became a noted parapsychologist who experimented with both clairvoyance and extrasensory effects on children.

Adams and Dixon Compared

Like the late Jeane Dixon, Adams earned her popularity by way of a dramatically accurate prophecy. Both astrologers associated with the most notable people of their day, predicted the imminent death of a country's leader, wrote very popular articles and books, used the most effective media of the day to promote themselves, and were the targets of skeptics. Even while both greatly popularized horoscopes in their day, they differed in that Dixon placed much emphasis on religion, while Adams focused on elevating astrology to the level of a science. Adams's heroic fight to earn respect for astrology can surely be seen as a link to the spirit of her ancestors, the country's pioneering revolutionaries.

John William Dunne

The Dream Weaver

1875-1949

Those who dance are considered insane by those who can't hear the music.

— George Carlin, *Brain Droppings*, 1997

When we say we hope our dreams come true, most of us simply mean that we want to reach our goals someday. But what if, when you awoke, you found that the things you had dreamed the night before had not only come true, but were emblazoned in the newspaper headlines? This is what happened not once, but time after time, to Englishman John William Dunne.

Like many of the other prophets in this book, Dunne was a complex man of many interests and talents. While little is known about his early life, he distinguished himself in adulthood by fighting as a British soldier. He became a pilot and a pioneer in aeronautical engineering, designing Britain's first military airplane. Yet he made a name for himself as much by what took place while he was sleeping as by any feats he accomplished while awake.

Over the course of his life, Dunne claimed to have vivid dreams in which certain details bore an uncanny resemblance to actual events that happened later. Dunne himself recorded thirty years of these remarkable foresights in his book, *An Experiment with Time* (1927).

The Stuff of Dreams

Dunne's first experience with precognition occurred while he was serving as an officer in the British army's Sixth Mounted Infantry during the second of the Boer Wars (1899–1902). This particular conflict, waged between British colonists and Dutch settlers (known as Afrikaners) in South Africa, was won by the British, paving the way for South Africa's unification in 1910.

In 1901, Dunne was sent to the Italian Riviera to recuperate from his battle wounds. One night, he dreamed he was back in Africa in a dusty Sudanese town, watching the arrival of three ragged explorers. The next day he read in a news headline that the paper had sent an overland expedition to Khartoum, Sudan. The story's description of the men's poor physical condition caused by their difficult journey was so similar to what he had seen in his dream that he was convinced he had some kind of psychic knowledge of the men's arrival.

In 1902, Dunne was encamped with the rest of his troop in a remote outpost, where it took some time for newspapers and mail to arrive from England. One night, Dunne had what he later described as an "unusually vivid and rather unpleasant" dream. He remembered standing on an island run by the French and feeling the ground cracking under his feet. In his dream he was shouting, "It's the island! Good

Lord, the whole thing is going to blow up!" The last thing he remembered was begging someone named Monsieur le Maire, "Listen, 4,000 people will be killed unless...."

In his *An Experiment with Time* (1934), Dunne describes the dream:

> I had memories of reading about Karakatoa, where the sea, making its way into the heart of a volcano ... blew the whole mountain to pieces. Forthwith, I was seized with a frantic desire to save the 4,000 (I knew the number) unsuspecting inhabitants.... I was at a neighboring island, trying to get the incredulous French authorities to dispatch vessels ... to remove the inhabitants of the threatened island.

According to Dunne, when newspapers finally did arrive at his camp, a *Daily Telegraph* article detailed the tragic eruption of Mount Pele on the French colony of Martinique. The headline read: "Volcano disaster in Martinique. Town swept away. An avalanche of flame. Probable loss of over 40,000 lives."

As happened in the dream, many survivors were taken by boat to a nearby island. However, Dunne dreamed of 4,000 inhabitants, which fell far short of the 40,000 casualties mentioned in the actual newspaper account. He explained to his friends at the time the article appeared that he misread it, and thought it actually did mention 4,000. It was only fifteen years later, he said, that he noticed the discrepancy between what he thought was printed in the paper and what was actually noted in the story.

The *World Almanac* lists the 1902 eruption as causing 28,000 deaths, far fewer than originally reported. It's interesting to note that a few days before the Martinique disaster, on April 24, an eruption at Santa Maria, Guatemala, took one thousand lives. But no combination of the numbers involved equals the number of people given in Dunne's dream.

However, a footnote in the *World Almanac* concerning the 1,000 deaths in Guatemala says that "An additional 3,000 deaths due to a malaria outbreak are sometimes attributed to the [Guatemala] eruption." This additional figure, added to the 1,000 could symbolize the total of the 4,000 mentioned by Dunne. However, this would not explain Dunne's "French connection" when it comes to this prediction.

Keith Ellis, author of *Prediction and Prophecy*, points out that "The fact that Dunne admits the error makes his story all the more credible, but suggests that he had foreknowledge of the newspaper story rather than of the event itself." Dunne himself admits that he could have read the newspaper story first and then been an unwitting victim of "identifying paramnesia." This occurs when the victim sees something and then imagines that he dreamed it. After this revelation, Dunne tried to eliminate identifying paramnesia by writing down his dreams immediately upon awakening.

Breaking the Boundaries of Time

Dunne was convinced that he had no special gift. Instead he believed that almost everyone had the power to dream future events and tell others what was going to happen—if they would learn to write down their dreams right after they had occurred. He considered dreams the backdrop against which past and present images come together to foretell the future, if only people would have the patience to analyze them.

Dunne's ideas about the function of dreams were closely related to his theories about time. He believed that time isn't a series of events that happen one after another, in a linear fashion, and then never occur again. Instead, he thought of time as multidimensional, where people's experiences draw on the past, present, and future all at once. In other words, when someone dreams of something before it has been reported, the event has, on some level, already happened. His idea of nonlinear time has been shared by many before and since, including Albert Einstein.

The Burden of Proof

Dunne tried hard to pass on his talent of dream prophecy to others. He taught his system of recording dreams to a small circle of friends and relatives. His book *An Experiment with Time* enjoyed considerable popularity and critical acclaim when it was first published. Evidently he was taken seriously enough for a while that in 1922, the British Society for Psychical Research performed a series of experiments based on his dream-recording system. To his dismay, however, none of the subjects tested showed any evidence of clairvoyance. Perhaps in an effort to salvage the study, Dunne volunteered himself as a subject—and proceeded to have a series of utterly disappointing dreams that seemed unlinked to any actual events without a great deal of imaginative "stretching." Despite his best efforts, he had trouble sustaining public enthusiasm for his theories.

The problem of interpretation

Pinning actual events to the shadowy images in a dream is a difficult task. Dreams are highly symbolic and subject to many personal biases by the dreamer and the listener. What one person interprets as meaning one thing could be taken quite differently by someone else. Still, people throughout the ages have been fascinated by dream prophecies and have even credited them with changing the course of history and people's lives.

After the sinking of the *Titanic* in 1912, dozens of accounts of prophetic dreams came out of the woodwork. One English businessman, J. Connon Middleton, actually was booked on the voyage until he had a dream about ten days before the ship launched. He saw the ship floating, keel up, with the crew swimming around it. The dream left him feeling despondent, and he canceled his reservation. In this case, paying attention to a dream proved to be a much better lifesaver than many on the ship were able to cling to.

Dreams also have been used in high-profile criminal investigations, such as the kidnapping of the Lindbergh baby in 1932. In that case, a group of Harvard psychologists actually asked the public to send in their dreams about the baby's whereabouts. Out of 1,300 responses, only 7 seemed to come anywhere close to the actual tragic outcome—that the baby would be found dead, buried in a ditch. Sadly, no amount of dreaming could change the future in this case.

Clearly, the errors and omissions in Dunne's dreams led many people to discount him. But the depth of his thoughts and work on the subject of dream precognition is worth noting. The history of this type of prophecy owes a great deal to this prolific dreamer.

EDGAR CAYCE
The Sleeping Prophet
1877-1945

*When there has been in the earth those groups that have
sufficiently desired and sought peace, peace will begin. It
must be within [the] self.*

— Edgar Cayce, (from reading 3976-28, courtesy of
the Association for Research and Enlightenment)

As we saw in the chapter on John Dee, Kenneth
Mackenzie, and others, some prophets were thought
to have received their gifts from a spirit sent from
the beyond. According to some accounts, Edgar Cayce (pro-
nounced KAY-see) was called to prophecy by the gentle
spirit of a woman in the woods, when he was only thirteen.

In this version of the story, Cayce was reading the Bible
in the woods near his family home in Hopkinsville, Kentucky.
All of a sudden he became aware of a strange woman standing in front of him. She had been sent in answer to his
prayers, she said, and asked what he wanted most in the
world. Although terrified, he told her that he wanted to be

helpful to others, especially sick children. The woman then disappeared, but as Cayce's life took shape and his healing talents became evident, there were a great many signs that he had been blessed with supernatural gifts.

Cayce has been called America's greatest psychic and the father of the New Age Movement. A prolific healer, clairvoyant, spiritualist, and devout believer in God, Cayce was both a brilliant man and a mass of contradictions. During his lifetime he was criticized by the medical community and ridiculed for his failed prophecies. Yet his beliefs are still going strong—in fact, today they appear to be catching fire again more than a half-century after his death. In 1997, the Association for Research and Enlightenment, founded to carry on his work, numbered 30,000 members.

Prolific Healer

First and foremost, Cayce was a healer. For more than forty years he diagnosed patients, gave prognoses, prescribed cures, and performed healings. In almost every case, patients were satisfied with his treatments.

Why is this so miraculous? Cayce practiced on thousands of patients over the course of his life without even touching them—by diagnosing and prescribing for patients mostly through mental telepathy while in a trance. What's more, he wasn't even a high school graduate, let alone a physician with an M.D. degree.

Cayce's Early Life

Cayce was born on a Kentucky farm in 1877. Among the prophets profiled here, Andrew Jackson Davis and Evangeline Adams were his closest contemporaries. Critic Dale Beyerstein states that Cayce knew of Davis. He "was aware of the Poughkeepsie seer . . . and Cayce's sessions resembled those of that mid-nineteenth-century 'wonder' more and more as Cayce got older." Like Christian Science founder Mary Baker Eddy, faith healer Joel Goldsmith, and psychic Jeane Dixon, Cayce was a devout Christian. He recalled reading all the books of the Bible once a year when he was a boy.

Cayce was never a good student, and he dropped out of high school after the ninth grade. His problems were caused, in part, by a learning disability that made him a poor speller. When he was nine years old he failed a spelling test. His father, a stern peace officer, was determined to teach him the lessons in the book, and took him aside for a grueling tutorial. Young Edgar, struggling to learn the word "cabin," heard a voice that told him, "Sleep now, and we will help you." He talked his father into letting him take a quick nap. He fell asleep, using his spelling book as a pillow. After only a few minutes he was awakened by his father, who quickly found that the boy knew every lesson in the book by heart—even down to which words were on a given page. After that, Cayce began taking his books to bed with him, seemingly memorizing them through osmosis. Thus began his spiritual journey as the "sleeping prophet," a nickname given to him later by a syndicated Hearst newspaper.

Cayce recalled another childhood experience during a game of baseball when he was knocked unconscious by a pitch. When he woke up, the normally passive and shy Cayce threw a temper tantrum. That night when he went to sleep, he began to speak as if in a trance. He guided his mother to the emergency care he needed to treat his condition, which he said was shock. Step by step, he instructed her to make and apply a poultice out of cornmeal, onions, and herbs, which cured him. The "sleeping prophet" was already beginning his unorthodox medical career.

Relatives and friends noticed that young Cayce had special powers, including the ability to see auras around people.

But his unique healing talents were not truly appreciated until he was twenty-one. At that time, Cayce was just starting to make his way as an apprentice photographer, and he hoped to marry his sweetheart, Gertrude Evans. In 1900, however, he lost his voice, and this strange malady persisted for months. Cayce was frustrated when doctors failed to heal him, so he turned to a local hypnotist and osteopath, Al Layne. When Layne began trying to put Cayce in a trance, Cayce told him there was no need—he could put himself to sleep and he proceeded to do so. Layne then made suggestions while Cayce launched into a highly technical, jargon-filled description of psychosomatic throat paralysis, based on being able to see inside his own body. When he awoke, he was cured.

Layne encouraged him to make greater use of his psychic gifts, but the humble and nervous Cayce at first resisted. He wasn't sure why he had these strange abilities, and because he was so deeply religious, he was concerned that they might have come from the devil. Also, he was afraid that he might hurt someone while trying to heal them.

Later, Cayce came to accept his strange calling, and resigned himself to a life of healings and psychic readings. Perhaps this is because he came to believe that in his trance state he was tapping into the Universal Unconscious, or the Universal Mind. When referring to the "akashic record" or what he called the "Book of Life," Cayce said it was the "record that the individual entity writes upon the skein of Time and Space, through patience, and opened when self has attuned to the Infinite, and may be read by those attuning to that consciousness." ("Akashic" describes a cosmic record that some psychics claim to be able to access.)

With only a few years of formal schooling, Cayce supported himself humbly through a string of low-paying jobs. He went from apprentice photographer to file clerk to bookstore clerk to insurance salesman. He and Gertrude married and had two children. Eventually, the word spread about the "uneducated country bumpkin" and his amazing ability to prescribe cures while lying on a couch in a trance. He supported himself at this time as a studio photographer and a Sunday school teacher. In 1901, Cayce began giving readings for others. His years of widespread popularity began about the time that those of Andrew Jackson Davis (profiled earlier) were ending.

In 1906, Cayce attempted to prove to the medical community that his powers were legitimate. He allowed a friend to talk him into giving a reading witnessed by doctors. After he fell into a deep trance, reportedly, the doctors and the audience began to debate exactly what kind of state he was in, and whether or not it might just be a trick. They began to stick needles, and even a hat pin, into his arms, hands, and face. When that failed to rouse him, one man actually cut off a part of his fingernail. When Cayce awoke, he was in great pain, both physically and emotionally. He found this treatment so traumatizing that he swore he'd never subject himself to such testing again.

By the 1930s, he was giving two readings a day. Cayce would eventually give approximately fourteen thousand readings. For many years he refused to accept any payment for them. Finally, his wife convinced him to charge a nominal fee.

A Natural Healer

As mentioned earlier, Cayce, like Andrew Jackson Davis, was a medical clairvoyant. Often all he needed was the patient's name and address before prescribing treatment, which he did while lying on a couch in a trance. In a typical session his wife would read the patient's information aloud, and he would give his prognosis and prescription. Then a scribe would write down what Cayce said. During this trance he would speak of medical terminology and unconventional practices that he did not understand while awake. He also was capable of speaking in ancient or foreign languages while in this altered state. Cayce apparently remembered nothing about a session once he awoke from the trance. His gifts seem all the more amazing because Cayce did not even graduate from high school.

In 1910, *The New York Times Magazine* published a feature story about him with the unfortunate headline, "Illiterate Man Becomes a Doctor When Hypnotized." Despite the *Times*'s error (he could read and write, of course), the article appeared to boost Cayce's career, and soon he was performing his remote healing for people all over the world. It is estimated that Cayce successfully treated thousands of patients.

Although most of his readings centered on curing, Cayce later included his thoughts on religion, philosophy, dreams, and the afterlife, and made predictions about the future of individuals and the world.

As with Davis, another prophetic man with no formal training as a physician, the medical establishment officially dismissed Cayce's successes, no matter how well-documented. They argued that Cayce's achievements resulted from a "self-fulfilling prophesy": In other words, naive people wanted so badly to believe Cayce could heal them that they somehow made it happen. Critics such as magician James Randi and psychic Dale Beyerstein have tried to show that several, if not all, of these cures were questionable, if not harmful. The credentials of the "doctors" involved with some of Cayce's patients also have been challenged. Beyerstein points out that Cayce "had ample help mastering the jargon" through his affiliations with licensed practitioners.

Still, many physicians and other health and science professionals were astonished by the accuracy of the terminology Cayce used from several scientific fields, including anatomy, physiology, and pharmacology. Cayce himself believed he was somehow able to enter the minds of experts, physicians, scientists, and specialists, and then capture and relay their thoughts. Later he was to claim he might have acquired this knowledge in past lives.

Cayce never intended that his patients completely forego the professional supervision of a medical practitioner. On the other hand, he believed that faith in a Higher Power's ability to heal was the first requirement in securing good health.

He also was a firm believer in natural and alternative healing remedies, long before they became fashionable or accepted by mainstream medicine. His viewpoint was truly holistic, and included many wellness techniques such as massage, chiropractic manipulation, osteopathy, and soothing baths (hydrotherapy). Cayce also prescribed herbs, essential oils, drugs, tonics, and special diets. With each prescription, he focused on the causes and prevention of illness rather than on symptoms and onetime cures.

Cayce once prescribed Jerusalem artichokes, native to North America, for a diabetic patient. The plant was introduced into Europe in 1616 as a food source, and into China during the same century. However, it was years later that it was discovered that this plant could be used to make insulin. It could be that Cayce had seen literature describing Native American cultivation and usage of the plant; still, his use of such alternative medicines did put him ahead of his time.

In 1927, Cayce and his family moved to Virginia Beach, Virginia, where wealthy supporters paid for the construction of a small hospital where he could work. In 1931, Cayce's hospital was turned into the Association for Research and Enlightenment (ARE). Today the ARE still houses not only Cayce's vast library of readings, but also hosts gatherings of like-minded individuals who come to nurture their spirituality and health through Cayce's natural methods. Visitors to the ARE can undergo a variety of the natural and alternative therapies that Cayce once advocated, including castor oil packs, foot reflexology, colonics, and massage therapy.

As Cayce's notoriety grew, his practices came under the watchful eye of authorities. He was arrested twice—once for practicing medicine without a license and once for "fortune-telling." The latter incident occurred during a visit to New York. Two women approached Cayce and asked for a reading. When he agreed, they revealed themselves to be police officers. As was the case with Evangeline Adams in 1914, all charges were eventually dropped. The magistrate on the case decided that the ARE was an incorporated ecclesiastical body and, as such, held religious beliefs that were outside the jurisdiction of the law.

Cayce's move to Virginia was not arbitrary. He believed that many areas of the world would be lost under water after the shift of the Earth's axis around the turn of the new millennium. Maps of the world (obtained from the ARE) as Cayce envisioned it show what will be left after the "inundation." Virginia "will be among the safety lands," he believed, which also included portions of Ohio, Indiana, and Illinois, much of the southern portion of Canada, and "the eastern portion of Canada."

Sins of the Past

After ten years of readings, Cayce gradually came to believe in reincarnation. He believed patients' present ills were caused by the sins they committed in their past lives, which resulted in negative *karma*. In Hinduism and Buddhism, karma, which is Sanskrit for "deeds," includes mental and physical acts that determine a person's destiny in the next life. Although there are many beliefs concerning reincarnation, Cayce basically believed that the soul, or one's essence, can return after death to inhabit a new physical form, whether human or animal.

Cayce's firmly held beliefs about reincarnation seem to defy the traditional Christian teachings about life after death, which he had held so dear in his youth. Nonetheless, he seemed quite comfortable with these contradictions.

Cayce said that he had lived previously as one of the first heavenly beings on Earth *before* the first man and woman, as an Egyptian priest named Ra-Ta (later deified as the god Ra), as a kinsman of the Apostle Paul named Lucius (Rom. 16:21), and as a Cornish mercenary in the British Army in 1752.

Contemporary psychic Alan Vaughan comments, "This strikes me as fanciful when compared with history. Why is it, one wonders, that 'past lives' so often come from colorful periods of history when the persons were important or rubbing shoulders with the great? How many Cleopatras, Napoleons, Caesars, Christs can there be?"

Cayce believed that he took his scientific knowledge with him from life to life, especially what he'd learned as a Grecian chemist living in ancient Troy. He thought that he might have been part of a group karma—a small community of people who keep reincarnating together through many ages.

Cayce believed in future lives, too. In 1936, he speculated that he would be reincarnated in A.D. 2100 and witness the rubble of New York City left by cataclysmic twentieth and twenty-first centuries.

Advice not Taken

There Is a River, Thomas Sugrue's biography of Cayce, appeared shortly before the psychic died in 1945. Ironically, this book boosted Cayce's popularity so much that it increased the number of requests for readings he received, contributing to fatigue and eventual collapse. At the time of his death, there was a backlog of three or four years of requests for his services.

Cayce admitted that his own readings told him not to do more than two readings for others a day. Yet he eventually increased that number to four or even six a day until he collapsed from exhaustion. After trying for several weeks to recuperate, he told friends that he would be "healed" on January 5, 1945. They interpreted this to mean that he expected to die on that day, but he died two days earlier, on January 3. Gertrude, Cayce's wife of forty-two years, died three months later.

Psychic Ability

According to Cayce, psychic ability is an extension of faith and love. These virtues can express themselves through significant dreams, premonitions, precognition, and the like. Just as we are each creative to varying degrees, so the higher forms of that creativity could be psychokinesis and other psychic phenomena. The reference book *Harper's Encyclopedia of Mysticism and Paranormal Experience* (1991) states that "Cayce said that if the mind and will are directed toward shared creativity, then resources will be drawn from the soul to yield helpful psychic impulses needed for those tasks. A person who has purity of heart and enduring love toward others will always have a ready supply of psychic energy available."

Cayce's Predictions

The following predictions illustrate Cayce's accuracy. As with the list of predictions made by Leonardo or Jeane Dixon, this list is far from comprehensive. Unlike the ambiguous verses of Nostradamus, or the somewhat vague warnings of Dunne, Cayce's statements were usually straightforward and clear, as were those of Jeane Dixon and Alan Vaughan. (A note of explanation: The numbers listed after a cited reading identify first the individual for whom the reading was given, and which reading it was. For example, a reading followed by "1431–4" would be the fourth reading given for client number 1,431.)

Stock market crash of 1929

In March 1929, Cayce was approached by Morton Blumenthal, one of the men who provided financial backing for Cayce's hospital. Blumenthal was troubled by a dream in which someone had told him to sell all his stocks. "I saw a bull following my wife, who was dressed in red," he told Cayce. The psychic went into a trance, and in his reading he told Blumenthal that he was receiving an impression of a downward movement of long duration—one allowing a great deal of latitude for those usually considered safe. Cayce's recommendation: "Dispose of all held," even box stocks, which were considered safe at the time (137–115).

On April 6, 1929, Blumenthal recounted another dream to Cayce where a gangster was grilling Blumenthal about whether or not he had murdered a man, and if anyone else knew. Cayce interpreted this to mean a fight going on in the Reserve Board caused by stock stimulation. His interpretation, also given in a reading, was this: "There must surely come a break where there will be panic in the money centers, not only of Wall Street's activity, but a closing of the boards in many other centers. . . . high and low quotations to continue for several moons while adjustments are being made" (137–117).

World War II

Cayce's predictions regarding World War II are some of the most dramatic and accurate illustrations of his sixth sense. One story goes that one day in July 1931 he was gardening in his yard. Suddenly, he dropped his hoe, ran into the house, and locked himself in the study. After several hours he emerged to tell of this vision: A world war was coming, and millions of men and women would be killed.

In fact, some forty-five million people lost their lives in that war. During the 1930s, he was to give thousands of sleep readings that contained accurate dates and descriptions related to World War II.

Appearance of new lands

Cayce's prediction of new lands in the Atlantic and Pacific Oceans may refer to the discovery in 1974 of parts of the island of Poseidon off the Bimini Islands. Moira Timms, in *Beyond Prophecies and Predictions* (1994), points out that "Poseidon is apparently one of the five residual islands from submerged Atlantis." She mentions that the 1974 discovery is "exactly where Cayce had predicted."

Interestingly, Cayce's prediction of an event at a nearly exact location in the vastness of the ocean is reminiscent of the almost exact placement by Jules Verne of the location where a space capsule would land. However, in contrast to the comparatively blank slate on which Verne wrote, people of Cayce's generation knew that geographers were studying patterns of geographical shifts based on past records and very measurable events.

Other predictions

The following are considered Cayce's successful predictions:

- ✧ Beginning and end of both world wars—1914–1918 and 1939–1945
- ✧ Stock market crash followed by the Great Depression (1929) and American political revival (1933)
- ✧ Independence of India (1947)
- ✧ Independence of Israel (1948)
- ✧ Death of President Franklin D. Roosevelt (1945)
- ✧ Death of President John F. Kennedy (1963)
- ✧ Discovery of the Dead Sea Scrolls (1947–1949)

- Invention of the laser (developed in 1960)
- A major hurricane in Japan (1959, 1967)
- A major earthquake in California (1906, 1933, 1971, 1989, 1994)
- A major tidal wave in the Philippines (1926)

Prophecies of Future Events

Cayce's prediction of the Second Coming of Christ in 1998, along with what he believed would be that year's cataclysmic events, is no doubt his most important prophecy. Here is a quotation from one reading in which he mentions the date specifically. When asked whether a date could be given to indicate the beginning of the Aquarian Age, he replied, "We will begin to understand fully in '98."

Another of his readings that hinted that 1998 would be significant in terms of the Second Coming following world-wide calamity is this: "The earth will be broken up in the western portion of America. The greater portion of Japan must go into the sea. . . . There will be shifting then of the poles. . . . And these will begin in those periods in '58 to '98, when these will be proclaimed as the periods when His light will be seen again in the clouds." (3976–15)

Polar or political shifts?

Followers of Cayce today generally express enthusiastic and unqualified support for his prophecies, except in one important area. Cayce's conviction concerning the shifting of the poles and the major changes in the earth's geography brought some criticism from various quarters. Specifically, he wrote:

> The polar axis of the earth will shift before 2001. This will transform our relationship to the sun. There will be radical changes in the earth's surface before 1998.

The greater change . . . will be in the North Atlantic seaboard. Watch New York! Connecticut and the like. (311-9)

Stuart Dean of ARE Press adds this qualification:

In fact, half of the people here don't even expect this kind of thing to take place, but think it will all manifest in the areas of consciousness, social life, and so forth. For example, the many earth-change predictions Cayce made in 1932 for 1936 were, without exception, manifested politically rather than geologically. The other half at the ARE, however, *does* believe that some form of *physical* change will be occurring. Who knows? Both could be right.

Other Cayce prophecies not fulfilled as predicted, in the process of being fulfilled, or as yet unrealized include:

- ✧ Democracy will replace Communism in China.
- ✧ Democracy will gradually develop in Russia.
- ✧ Democracy will spread throughout the world.
- ✧ Flooding of the coasts will begin in 1998.
- ✧ "Portions of the now East Coast of New York, or New York City itself, will in the main disappear." (1152–11)
- ✧ Los Angeles and San Francisco will be destroyed even before New York. (1152–11)
- ✧ Large land areas will suddenly disappear below the ocean, among them northern Europe, southern Alabama, North and South Carolina.
- ✧ California will fall into the Pacific Ocean.
- ✧ An area opposite the South Pacific will sink and rise.*
- ✧ The greater portion of Japan will be destroyed by earthquakes and volcanic eruptions.
- ✧ The Great Lakes will flow through the Mississippi Valley and empty into the Gulf of Mexico.

- The world's food source will become "portions of Saskatchewan ... the Pampas area of the Argentine ... portions of South Africa ... portions of Montana and Nevada." (3651-1)
- Three repositories of the records of the Atlantean civilization will be discovered (in Egypt, Bimini, and the Yucatán), perhaps by 1998.
- World War III will erupt in 1999. Within a year of the start of this war, civilization as we know it will end.
- New lands will appear in the Atlantic and Pacific Oceans. (See also fulfilled predictions above.)

*Concerning the area opposite the South Pacific that Cayce predicted would sink and rise, Timms points out that, as far back as 1959, "A Reuters dispatch from Athens reported water levels in several Greek towns had dropped, exposing the seabed in places and beaching craft in mud."

More recently, the sea level of the Caspian Sea began sinking in 1975, leading the former Soviet Union to undertake a fifty-year project involving blasting a canal east of the Ural Mountains in what Russians would call "the grandest engineering project of all time."

Failed Predictions

Like other prophets, Cayce failed with many of his prophecies. Critics have compiled lists of these failures, especially those that are dramatically wrong.

For example, though Cayce offered many suggestions to Charles Lindbergh (1902–1974) in 1932 concerning the kidnapping of his son, his information proved useless. Cayce also predicted that by 1968 most people in China would have converted to Christianity. However, China today remains officially atheist, while Buddhism and Taoism are the traditional religions of the people. Other Chinese people are considered folk religionists.

The New Age

In 1931, Japanese mystic Meishu Sama (1882–1955) said that he had revelation that the New Age of light had begun on June 15 of that year. Less than a year later, Cayce, too, declared that the New Age had just begun. This is the period astrologers call the Age of Aquarius, much sung about in the 1970 rock musical *Hair*. It is also the Golden Age or the New Order of the Ages referred to in Mayan and Babylonian prophecies. Leonardo and Nostradamus both made imaginative reference to the so-called "last days." Other prophets, including Cayce and Jeane Dixon, use descriptions that are more obviously influenced by Scripture, especially the Book of Revelation. Similar to the Book of Exodus, the Book of Revelation is often called by the major event that it describes—the Apocalypse.

A Man of Destiny

According to Cayce, people are largely responsible for their own destinies. In 1935 he made this statement (the completely capitalized words are his, and are apparently for emphasis):

> Tendencies in the hearts and souls of men are such that these [good or bad things] may be brought about. For... it is not the world, the earth, the environs about it nor the planetary influences, nor the associations or activities, that RULE man, RATHER does man by HIS COMPLIANCE with divine law bring ORDER out of chaos; or, by his DISREGARD of the associations and laws of the divine influence, bring chaos and DESTRUCTIVE forces into his experience.

JEANE DIXON

America's Best-Known Prophet

1918-1997

I believe that everything upon this earth has at one time or another been alive. Therefore, there's nothing new, is there?

— Jeane Dixon, 1968

J eane Dixon will always be remembered for one prediction most people wish had never come true: that President John F. Kennedy would die while in office.

In 1952, Dixon, a devout Catholic, was praying before a statue of the Virgin Mary in St. Matthew's Cathedral in Washington, D.C. According to her recollection, she saw the church lit by a brilliant image of the White House. Hovering above the presidential residence were four shimmering numbers: 1, 9, 6, and 0. She saw a young man with blue eyes and brown hair standing on the threshold of the White House. Her inner voice told her that this man was a Democrat who would be elected president in 1960, but tragically, would die while in office.

In another vision before the assassination, Dixon said she saw black hands, apparently representing death. The hands were removing the nameplate from Vice President Lyndon Johnson's office door.

It is said that all adult Americans who were around on November 22, 1963, remember what they were doing when they heard "the news." The story is often told that on the day Kennedy was shot, Dixon was at the Mayflower Hotel in Washington, lunching with friends. Those who were with her remember that Dixon became so distraught she couldn't eat, saying, "Something dreadful is going to happen to the president today."

Suddenly, the musicians performing for the diners stopped playing. Their conductor announced that he had just been told that someone had shot *at* the president in Dallas. Dixon sobbed. Her friends tried to comfort each other, suggesting that the president surely was not seriously hurt. "No," Dixon said, "the president is dead. You will learn that he is dead."

A Popular Prophet

Though perhaps not a household name, psychic, writer, and Sun Sign astrologer Jeane Dixon remains one of the best-known modern-day "prophets." Her frequent appearances on television and her articles in newspapers and tabloids made her, if not an authority, at least a recognized and sought-after predictor of events.

During her life and long career in the public eye, Dixon drew her share of critics, as well. But the fact remains that to many she was a popular and respected visionary, who benefited from the media coverage available in our modern age. She was certainly not the least of prophets; several of her many predictions actually came true. Although some of what Dixon predicted might be considered off-the-wall, much of what she foresaw can be attributed to a mixture of good judgment, common sense, and a keen awareness of current events.

Still, Dixon continues to be a persistent target of critics of the paranormal. Magician and author James Randi, who has made it part of his life's work to debunk psychic claims, found her an especially easy target. In his book, *The Mask of Nostradamus*, Randi tells the reader to turn to a particular page for a "complete list of [Dixon's] correct prophecies." When you turn to that page, however, it's blank. Randi also took issue with the methods of Uri Geller, famous particularly for bending metal objects by psychokinesis. Randi was even known to follow Geller around, repeating Geller's feats after he was finished to show that they were tricks and not truly produced by special powers.

Dixon herself was a good sport when it came to criticism. She once said, "I love skeptics, because they are so interesting to work with. The more you give the better life is; so you can give the skeptic a great deal more than you can give someone who has already accepted the true spiritual world." In fact, much of what Dixon said seemed designed to be provocative. She knew that the popular press always finds controversy interesting.

Dixon's Early Life

Jeane Pinckert was born in Medford, Wisconsin, in 1918, one of seven children of German immigrants. She grew up in Santa Rosa, California, and attended a Catholic high school in Los Angeles. As a young girl, she imagined herself someday entering a convent. But she also thought she would like to be an actress. Throughout her life she may have become a little of each as she mixed elements of both religion and theatricality into secular prophecy.

Even though young Jeane was raised Catholic, she was strangely drawn to soothsayers. Although the church officially frowns on building spiritual faith on the occult, there are Catholic astrologers, even among the priesthood. A Jesuit priest named Father Henry, who practiced divination through numerology, palmistry, and astrology, among others, assured the young Jeane that she did indeed have a gift. He told her that he thought she would someday hold the hands of famous people and enjoy acclaim herself. Father Henry became her mentor in astrology.

According to her own recollection, when Dixon was eight years old, a soothsayer saw that the lines in the child's palm formed the six-pointed shape of the star of David. A multi-pointed star was seen in her other palm. The fortune-teller concluded that the girl had a gift for prophesying. Jeane's mother took this prediction seriously and encouraged her daughter to use her gift. The soothsayer gave the girl a gift— a crystal ball. Dixon described the crystal she used as "not just glass, but mined crystal, a semiprecious stone." She later deemed it unnecessary, however, to her ability to predict the future. Dixon's family also recalls that young Jeane showed evidence of precognition. At times she would predict the content of letters that had not yet arrived.

Both the priest and fortune-teller were right. By the time she was fourteen, Jeane was predicting the future for others, especially for entertainment celebrities. Astrologer Evangeline Adams also focused on celebrities from early in her career. Both women realized that the dramatic aspects of prophecy could feed a celebrity-hungry public.

Power Source

Dixon implied several times in her life that she thought some of her prophecies were revelations from God. In interviews and in her writings, she said she received her impressions not only through prayer and meditation but also through telepathy, touching hands, psychometry, scrying, dreams, and visions. She said she could sense a vision coming about three days beforehand. While she prepared for the day, and on the day itself, she normally felt inspired and buoyant. Her visions were sometimes accompanied by music and voices, and appeared either in color or black and white. For instance, she said that she once saw red boots, which she presumed were symbolic of the devil, walking a few inches above an altar.

Dixon had a simple but apparently sincere approach to religion, as seen in her reflections *Reincarnation and Prayers to Live By* (1970), *The Call to Glory* (1971), *Yesterday, Today, and Forever* (1976), and *A Gift of Prayer: Words of Comfort and Inspiration* (1995). Dixon also published the entertaining *Astrological Cookbook* in 1976 and an amusing *Horoscope for Dogs* in 1979.

Dixon was altruistic, as well, and founded Children to Children, a nonprofit organization to help children of the world. She also extended her outreach efforts to adults, rarely missing an opportunity to encourage people to pray.

The Seeress of Washington

In 1934, Jeane Pinckert became Jeane Dixon when she married James Dixon, a Pinckert family friend and a partner in automobile sales with the pioneering movie producer Hal Roach (1892–1992). Roach was one of many influential people the Dixons came to know.

At the outbreak of World War II, the Dixons moved to Washington, D.C. In this socially active and politically alert community, Jeane, an articulate and charming woman, found that her predictions were becoming more political in nature.

Her reputation for accuracy quickly spread beyond her local circle, and she became known as "the Seeress of Washington."

After the war, James Dixon organized his own real estate firm, and his wife joined him as a broker. Together, they specialized in finding facilities in the capital for foreign embassies. The business helped to shield her somewhat from the many requests for predictions she received daily. At the same time, her social and business connections in Washington would sometimes provide very credible witnesses to her prophecies. Her prediction about the first space satellite, for example, was made on a television show with Joseph E. Davies present as a fellow guest. Davies was U.S. ambassador to the Soviet Union from 1936 to 1938 and ambassador to Belgium during 1938 and 1939.

On the Pulse of Current Events

Dixon's most notable predictions forecast some of the most significant events of the twentieth century. She was an intelligent woman, with a good grasp of past and current world events. She also was a keen observer of the cycles of history. As with many historians and academics of her day, these qualities helped her make educated judgments.

In 1959, the opinion widely held in Dixon's Washington circle was that it was time for a Democratic president, so her assertion that a Democrat would be elected was as much common sense as visionary. Dixon knew how to integrate her Sun Sign astrology with such general forecasts by her contemporaries.

While her earliest predictions were private, Dixon gained a large following rather quickly through the mass media, as did Evangeline Adams. She finally gained international recognition through her world-syndicated Sun Sign astrology column, which began in 1946 after she had gained popularity as a prophet. However, her astrological commentaries were not recognized for authenticity by many, if any, certified astrologers. Dixon also wrote and co-wrote books.

But it was Dixon's 1947 prediction of the partition of India down to the very day, one month before it happened, that earned her worldwide attention. While this could be another example of getting down to specifics about what was already a widely held opinion, predicting the very day was fairly amazing and caused people to take her more seriously.

While speculating on political coups and the deaths of those who were already old or sick could be relatively easy, no amount of speculation could explain her uncanny predictions about certain individuals. How was it that on the day of actress Carol Lombard's fatal airplane crash, Dixon predicted that it was unsafe for the actress to fly?

Dixon's Predictions: Right, Wrong, and Pending

While scholars have yet to compile and evaluate a truly comprehensive list of Dixon's predictions that would show her original wording and the dates her prophecies were made, as well as whether and when the events took place, the following abbreviated list is based on the most reputable sources available at this time. Similar or related prophecies are grouped together, while others are listed chronologically by the year an event took place. They are not given in the order in which Dixon made the predictions.

At times Dixon rethought what she had foretold, which often led to new and usually more precise predictions. Commentary is given later in this chapter on items marked with an asterisk (*).

Events predicted accurately

- ❖ It was unsafe for actress Carole Lombard to travel by airplane. She died in an airplane crash that very night. (1942)
- ❖ President Franklin D. Roosevelt had only a few months to live. He died a few months after this prediction. (1945)
- ❖ Winston Churchill, then prime minister of England (1939–1945), would not win the upcoming election. He lost to Clement Attlee in July 1945.
- ❖ Churchill would come back into power later. He was again prime minister from 1951 to 1955.
- ❖ India was to gain its independence and partition. Both happened in 1947.
- ❖ Mahatma Gandhi would be assassinated. He was, in 1948.
- ❖ The Korean War (1950–1953) would end in a stalemate.
- ❖ Joseph Stalin (1879–1953) would die in 1953.
- ❖ Stalin's replacement would be Georgy Malenkov (1953).
- ❖ Malenkov would be replaced two years into his reign by a "portly military man with wavy hair, green eyes, and a goatee." This aptly described Malenkov's replacement, Marshal Nikolai Bulganin, premier from 1955 to 1958.
- ❖ Nikita Khrushchev (1894–1971), who served at the helm of the Soviet government from 1956 to 1964, would rise quickly to power and then fall into disfavor. He did both.
- ❖ A "silver ball" would be launched into space during Khrushchev's rule. The satellite *Sputnik* was launched in 1957.
- ❖ U.S. Secretary of State John Foster Dulles would die in 1959.
- ❖ There would be race riots in the United States during the 1960s.

- U.N. Secretary-General Dag Hammarskjöld would die in a plane crash in 1961.
- Marilyn Monroe would commit suicide. She apparently did, in 1962.
- President John F. Kennedy would die while in office. He did, in 1963.*
- The first two letters of John F. Kennedy's assassin were "OS," and the last letter was possibly a "D." This description fits the name of [Lee Harvey] Oswald.
- There would be a major Alaskan earthquake in 1964.
- Martin Luther King, Jr. would be assassinated. He was, in 1968.
- Three astronauts in a space capsule would die in a fire on the ground. This happened in 1967.
- U.S. Senator Robert Kennedy would be assassinated. He was, in 1968.
- Richard M. Nixon would be president. She predicted this some twenty years before his election in 1968.
- There would be a government wiretapping scandal by 1971. Dixon was close, but slightly off, on this one— Watergate events began in 1972.
- There would be an attempted assassination of Governor George Wallace. There was, in 1972.
- There would be improved relations between the United States and China. Nixon first visited China in 1972.

Events predicted incorrectly

- Nixon would appoint five Supreme Court justices. Here again she was close, but not perfectly accurate: He appointed only four.
- Nixon's presidency would survive the Watergate scandal.
- Nixon would make a political comeback as president in 1976.
- Russia would put the first man on the moon. The United States did, in 1969.
- Russia would move into Iran in 1953.

- Russia would move into Palestine in 1957.
- Dwight Eisenhower would not run for president in 1956. He ran and won.
- World War III would begin in 1958.
- Red China would start World War III in 1958. In another prediction, she said this war would begin off the shores of the Chinese islands of Quemoy and Matsu.
- Red China would be admitted to the United Nations in 1959.
- Russia would move into Iran in 1960.
- Fidel Castro would fall from power in 1961.
- Fidel Castro would be "more than likely dead" by 1966. Castro was still in power as of 1998.
- The widowed Jacqueline Kennedy (1929–1994) would not remarry.
- The widowed Jacqueline Kennedy Onassis would remarry.
- Spiro Agnew would rise in stature politically. He resigned in disgrace from the vice presidency in 1973.
- Walter Reuther would run for president in 1964.
- The Vietnam War would end on August 5, 1966. It continued into 1975.
- In 1975 there would be an internal upheaval in the United States. The opposing forces would then cause similar upheavals in Africa, South America, and Southeast Asia. None of this happened.
- A comet would hit the earth in the 1980s, causing havoc, earthquakes, and tidal waves.*
- Senator Howard Baker would seek the presidency in 1980, but his enemies would try to discredit him because of a scandal.
- The largest civil war in U.S. history would take place in the 1980s. This did not happen.
- George Bush would be reelected president of the United States in 1992.

Predictions pending

Some of the more notable predictions made by Dixon that could still come true include the following, listed in random order. A strict chronology of the predicted events would be nearly impossible, since some events seem to cancel out others.

- ⟡ The United States will return to its former policy of armed preparedness.
- ⟡ Old civil defense shelters will be revived in the United States, as the world prepares for threatening disaster.
- ⟡ Food and energy resources will increase in Canada and Brazil, making these countries very powerful.
- ⟡ World scientists will unite to use knowledge about solar energy obtained from UFOs.
- ⟡ A "sun pill" will run machines. This "sun pill" will be of great health benefit to all.
- ⟡ A woman will be president of the United States.
- ⟡ The two-party system will vanish from American politics.
- ⟡ There will be a catastrophic world war in 1999.
- ⟡ There will be enormous fatalities from germ warfare.
- ⟡ There will be a wave of suicides in the United States.*
- ⟡ Parents will more often teach children at home, as schools and formal education virtually disappear.
- ⟡ Third World forces will attack the United States.
- ⟡ China will attempt world domination but ultimately will be defeated.
- ⟡ The dogmas of the Catholic Church will be attacked.
- ⟡ A pope will be assassinated.
- ⟡ The papacy will cease to exist.
- ⟡ A religious leader (born on February 5, 1962) will become the Antichrist.*
- ⟡ The geography of the earth will be totally altered by the year 2000.*
- ⟡ In 2020, the Antichrist will be revealed. Millions will perish during Armageddon, but good will triumph over

evil.* After Armageddon, the world will become a disease-free paradise with pollution-free cities. Humans will travel through space at the speed of light. Individual nations will keep their identity under a world government.

Dixon's Most Famous Prediction

Dixon's obituary in *The New York Times* noted the prediction for which she will always be most famous—the death of President John F. Kennedy while in office.

During the eleven years between her first vision at St. Matthew's in 1952 and November 22, 1963, the fateful day on which the president was assassinated, Dixon repeated her prophecy of JFK's death in office so often that it may be one of the most thoroughly documented of all prophecies. At some point Dixon changed the detail of "death while in office" to *assassination* while in office. She also later told James Grayson Bolen, in an interview for *Psychic* magazine, that "Sometimes I do get the exact time, as in the assassination of President Kennedy. That was a revelation; it was given to the exact day." However, Dixon first described the assassination-related visions to investigative journalist Jack Anderson, who published the conversations in a 1956 *Parade* magazine. Dixon always asserted that she actually told *Parade* that the president would not merely die in office but that he would be assassinated. According to Dixon, the magazine refused to print that very significant detail.

Dixon later related her Kennedy prophecy to parapsychologist F. Regis Riesenman. However, magician James Randi traced Dixon's various retellings of the vision, showing that—like so many fascinating stories—it grew more detailed each time.

On the other hand, probably the most important of Dixon's failed predictions are two that seem to contradict her vision of a president doomed to die in office. Before the JFK assassination, she predicted that someone other than Kennedy would be elected president in 1960. In yet another prediction, she said that Richard Nixon would win the 1960 election.

Despite these inconsistencies, Dixon made no secret of her strong premonition of tragedy ahead for JFK, and said she tried to warn him on several occasions. The Kennedys, however, would have paid little, if any, attention to an astrologer's advice. According to David Wallechinsky's *Book of Predictions* (1981), "The brash Kennedys had little use for psychics and a devil-may-care attitude about security."

In contrast, the Ronald Reagan White House was very receptive to astrologers, even if it did not always follow their advice. First Lady Nancy Reagan's fascination with astrologers (including Dixon), and her influence, in turn, on the president, was well-publicized by the popular press. In his autobiographical book *Where's the Rest of Me?* (1981), Ronald Reagan said that he and Nancy were close friends with Jeane Dixon.

During November of 1963, seven years after the Anderson interview, Dixon's friends noticed that she was becoming more and more anxious about JFK. Dixon said later that she had tried to warn the president through her contacts in the nation's capital specifically not to go to Dallas on that day. Her warning probably wasn't the only one—JFK's secretary also tried to discourage him from going to Dallas, apparently because of rumors of assassination plans. Perhaps Dixon's warnings were among those the secretary tried to relay.

Whether or not JFK had heard of Dixon's fears, he would not have been likely to change his plans, for reasons beyond just a distrust of astrologers. JFK's attitude toward assassination was apparently almost as fatalistic as Abraham Lincoln's.

Lincoln once told the author of the highly influential book *Uncle Tom's Cabin*, Harriet Beecher Stowe, "Whichever way the [Civil] war ends, I have the impression I shall not last long afterward [*sic*] it is over." He was, in fact, fatally shot on April 14, 1865, five days after the surrender of Robert E. Lee (1807–1870) at Appomattox. Likewise, JFK was quoted as saying, "If they want to get you, they're going to get you."

In his *Patterns of Prophecy* (1973), psychic Alan Vaughan, who tried unsuccessfully to warn Robert Kennedy that he, too, would be assassinated, offers an excellent survey of several individuals' efforts to warn Lincoln, JFK, Martin Luther King, Jr., and Robert Kennedy of their assassinations. Interestingly, Vaughan notes how each of these men mentioned his own assassination shortly before the fact.

Other Dixon Predictions

Sputnik

Dixon's description of the satellite she correctly predicted as a "silver ball" was uncharacteristically poetic, more reminiscent of the enigmatic style of Nostradamus. As mentioned in the chapter on Jules Verne, several prophetic science fiction writers foresaw satellites.

In fact, before Russia launched the first space satellite, *Sputnik*, in October 1957, satellites were rarely mentioned by prophets *other* than science fiction writers. During the following decade, however, general interest in satellites was expressed, but more as fictional imaginings than as prophecy.

The comet

Astrologer/architect A. T. Mann, in his *Millennium Prophecies*, dates Dixon's comet prediction to 1978. He assigns her prediction for the 1980s, specifically to 1985, apparently presuming she was thinking of the appearance of Halley's comet.

Dixon was not the first to envision a falling comet. The reference to "the great star" by Nostradamus (Century II, 91) is usually presumed to refer to Halley's comet as well. The comet itself was observed in 1682 by Edmund Halley (1656–1742). It was identified as the same one that had also been seen in 1531 and 1607.

In his *Patterns of Prophecy*, Alan Vaughan wondered, too, if Dixon had in mind Halley's comet, which the scientific community knew was due for a return visit in 1985. "It would be indeed surprising" if a comet would hit the earth, Vaughan commented, "since a comet is mainly composed of gas, (whereas) meteors would be more likely to cause such havoc."

Predictions for the New Millennium

The Antichrist revisited

Another Dixon prediction that she revised over time concerned a child who was to be born on February 5, 1962. This child would one day become a great religious leader, she said, whose power would grow greatly until 1999 (when the "child" would be thirty-seven.) In 1973, Alan Vaughan noticed that Dixon had changed her interpretation. She then said the child would be an Antichrist.

Dixon's concern about the Antichrist, Communist Russia, Red China, and enemies of her faith and country in general is consistent with themes of seers down through the centuries. The most notorious person of any period is thought to be the Antichrist or anti-savior. This has been true from the time of Nero, whom early Christians considered to be the Antichrist. Again, in the twentieth century, most of the civilized world considers Hitler the epitome of evil, and therefore the

Antichrist. Some Catholics at the time of the Protestant Reformation thought that Martin Luther was the Antichrist, while for some Protestants each pope, or the papacy collectively, is the Antichrist. For many nations, especially when religion is not separated from politics, religion's enemy is the devil, and the devil of devils is an anti-savior, usually the leader of the enemy. Of course, the enemy might claim the same.

Mass suicides

Shortly after the Heaven's Gate tragedy, cult expert Chip Berlet, who claims no psychic insight, said that the country could expect more mass suicides as the decade progressed. As the millennium approaches, the Political Research Associates are hearing about "thousands of these totalitarian groups with apocalyptic visions of reality.... As we approach the year 2000, with all its rotund significance, all kinds of religious movements are looking at it as a time of possible violence, or cataclysm, or mass suicide." "Rotund significance" refers to the importance that many people, especially the superstitious, attach to a "round" date, that is, one with two or three zeros in a row. Though Dixon does not mention mass suicide in relation to the millennium, it is possible that her prediction could still come true during the turn of the century.

An end to peace

In 1968, Jeane Dixon said that the false security of so-called disarmament will suddenly be broken by world war in 1999: "In thirty-two years [the years 1999–2000] there is going to be a *tremendous* happening.... And when this occurs, the Jewish people will say it is the coming of their Messiah and the Christians will say it is the Second Coming of Christ. I received it as a revelation." This prediction of world war and the coming of a Messiah echoes many other prophets' visions of what the new millennium will bring. Whether this "tremendous happening" occurs, and if so, ends up being for the good or detriment of humankind, however, remains to be seen.

Dixon's Legacy

When prolific writer George Sullivan was gathering material for his book *Work Smart, Not Hard* in 1987, he asked celebrities how they made their leisure time count. Dixon replied:

> I do not nor do I want to "get away from it all." Rather than getting away from it all, I relish staying with it, conquering it, and moving on to the next challenge.
>
> I believe that work is prayer and love in action. Approached that way, any task becomes ennobling. We need not be compulsive about our work to take delight in it and to see in its completion the fulfillment of God's plan for us as individuals.
>
> True happiness and peace comes from finding our mission and purpose in life. When we discover that, and pursue it, we do not tire nor become discouraged. Each new morning is a reborn world in which all our work can service the Lord who has given it to us.

Whether people view Dixon as a true seeress or as a mere entertainer, her media savvy and prolific career have ensured her place in popular astrology and the psychic world. Through her written legacy, Dixon continues to influence fans, especially those who enjoy her popular Sun Sign astrology. Her legacy lives on as we await the outcome of her pending prophecies.

ALAN VAUGHAN
The Most Successful Predictor
1936–

*To those who see no evidence of God in their lives,
I recommend that they explore their own patterns
of prophecy.*

— Alan Vaughan, *Patterns of Prophecy*, 1973

*[Unlike the other profiles in this book, the following is
based almost entirely on the author's own correspondence
with Vaughan since May 1997. –DW]*

W ho is the world's most accurate predictor of future events? Though many are familiar with the reputations of Nostradamus or Jeane Dixon, this badge of respect has been given to a man of our time—Alan Vaughan.

A Journey into the Supernatural

Vaughan had his first psychic experience in November 1965, when he was twenty-eight years old. At that time he was a science textbook editor in New York City, with a healthy skepticism for all things supernatural. Nonetheless, one day he began playing with a Ouija board. To his surprise, the board predicted that a terrible blizzard would strike New York, and gave exact dates for its beginning and end. As the Ouija predicted, on January 31 and February 1 a snowstorm dropped 102 inches of snow on upstate New York. One thousand cars were abandoned on the New York State throughway. A cover story in *Newsweek* published at the time called it the worst blizzard there in eighty years.

After that, Vaughan claimed the Ouija board caused him to be possessed for twenty-four hours by a spirit named Nada. During this time he wrote a message: "Each of us has a spirit while living. Do not meddle with spirits of the dead. It could lead to possession." Vaughan also remembers what he describes as "spiritual energy from my higher self, which flooded through me and pushed the possessing spirit out. At that moment I became 'psychic'—and could sense other dimensional realities."

Vaughan then burned the Ouija board. After a frightening night during which he saw phantoms stalking his bedroom, he decided it was time to find out how psychic phenomena worked. He began reading the classics of psychic research.

His Psychic Training and Research

Vaughan was awarded a grant from Eileen Garrett's Parapsychology Foundation to do research from 1967–68 into precognition and mediumship in England, Holland, and Germany.

Vaughan's first research project in England involved collecting hundreds of psychic readings from mediums, psychics, astrologers, fortune-tellers, tarot readers, crystal gazers, and other professional intuitives. He had hoped to witness these psychics prophesying the future, but he found that they could predict only *his* future—so he became their guinea pig in studies on precognition. A number of their predictions were fulfilled. For example, they said he would become a psychic and channeler himself and write books about psychic research. The participants in his study also predicted the number of children he would have (three) and that he would appear on television. At this writing Vaughan has appeared on about eighty television shows.

With the British medium Douglas Johnson as his teacher, Vaughan began his development as a psychic in London, at both the College of Psychic Studies and the Society for Psychical Research.

Speaking in "Tongues"

During this time, Vaughan investigated a case in which "Helen," an amateur medium, received messages one letter at a time while she was in trance. She would call out the letters to her roommate, and the two gradually compiled words. Vaughan describes in his book, *Doorways to Higher Consciousness* (1997), how he was able to identify the language Helen was using as Koine Greek, a language she certainly knew nothing about in her waking life. Koine was also used throughout the eastern Mediterranean world during the Hellenistic and Roman periods and was used in developing the New Testament. However, Vaughan's case had nothing to do with Scripture. Moreover, when the trance took hold, Helen could respond in Koine when asked questions in English.

Vaughan's research led him to understand that the entity communicating through Helen supplied poetry in Koine that described details of an ancient mystery cult that worshiped the Greek goddess Demeter. Vaughan explained why this was especially fascinating: "No one really knew the details of what went on [in the cult] because members were forbidden to reveal its secrets—on pain of death. So there is no published source to which the channeled poetry could be compared. By the same token, Helen could not have acquired this information in any normal way."

Even more important, Helen was displaying responsive "xenoglossy"—answering questions in an unstudied foreign language—and providing evidence of channeling a 2,000-year-old spirit. Andrew Jackson Davis and Edgar Cayce, as you may recall, also spoke in unlearned languages while in trances.

More Tragedy Foreseen for the Kennedys

In 1968, Vaughan began a research project into precognitive dreaming with Hans Bender, who died in 1993, at the Institute for Border Areas of Psychology in Freiburg, Germany. On several occasions, Vaughan stated in correspondence written during the three months leading up to Robert Kennedy's assassination that Kennedy would be shot within weeks. These included an April 20, 1968, memo to Bender and a May 25 letter to Stanley Krippner, the director of Maimonides Dream Laboratory in Brooklyn. Eleven days later, on June 5, 1968, Robert Kennedy was indeed assassinated by Sirhan Sirhan. In an interview with the author, Alan commented, "Premonitory dreams and synchronicity about Martin Luther King's assassination prompted me to write them."

Synchronicity is defined in *Webster's New World College Dictionary* (1997) as "the fact or state of being synchronous; simultaneous occurrence." In terms of prophecy, synchronicity is important because when many things come together at the same time, it leads to a conclusion of significance. Vaughan defines synchronicity as "meaningful coincidence." Of course, his theories on this are much more complex. At one point, Vaughan published twelve experimental tests of theories of synchronicity using dream telepathy. (These are described later in more detail.) His extensive research on synchronicity is the subject of his 1979 book *Incredible Coincidence*.

Becoming the World's Most Successful Predictor

In 1968 Robert Nelson established the Central Premonitions Registry (CPR), which was modeled after the British bureau. He was inspired to start this registry after reading Vaughan's letter to Krippner.

Over its twenty-year life, the CPR registered predictions from 3,500 people in twenty-eight countries. Based on this store of predictions, in 1981 the organization nominated Vaughan to the *Guinness Book of World Records* as "the world's most successful predictor." Shortly afterward, skeptics persuaded publishers of this well-known repository of fascinating facts to drop the ESP categories, and they were never reinstituted.

Vaughan's Predictions

Like other psychics, Vaughan has seen many of his predictions fulfilled. Other predictions have been less successful, while others are still pending.

Watergate scandal

Vaughan states that "After Nixon's election in November 1968, I registered a prediction with the Central Premonitions Registry on November 6, 1968, which stated: 'Enormous scandals in the Nixon administration will come to light in the second half of his administration.' " Few would disagree that the Watergate scandal qualifies as "enormous," and indeed the scandal did come to light during the period Vaughan predicted.

Floods on the East Coast

In a psychic experiment for researcher R. E. L. Masters on December 12, 1969, Vaughan predicted: "By 1972–1973, severe flooding will affect the Eastern Coast of the United States." He also registered this prediction with the CPR. In June 1972, Hurricane Agnes created record-breaking floods on the East Coast, killing 134 people and causing $1.7 billion in damages.

Attack on the Pope

On December 5, 1969, in another experiment for researcher Masters, Vaughan predicted: "A madman will attack the Pope in an attempt to kill him next year." A year later, on November 27, 1970, when the Pope visited the Philippines, he was attacked while at the Manila airport and wounded by a knife-wielding man whom the press described as "a madman." Notice that the prediction of a year before had five elements (the madman, the pope, an attack, the attempt to kill, next year), each of which came true.

The Columbia space shuttle launch schedule

After watching a television show on January 6, 1981, about the scheduled launch of the first space shuttle, *Columbia*, Vaughan wrote to the CPR and the Cable News Network (CNN) television program *Freeman Reports*: "The launch date will be closer to April 12 than the present schedule of March 17." The launching time of *Columbia* was later postponed, and then rescheduled. The new date coincided exactly with the date Vaughan mentioned three months before.

Challenger disaster

In Vaughan's 1982 book *The Edge of Tomorrow*, he wrote: "A shuttle launch will have severe malfunctions that could threaten the space program." Four years later, the tragic explosion of the *Challenger* on January 28, 1986, was initially termed "a major malfunction" by the National Aeronautical Space Administration (NASA). It was nearly three years before NASA launched another manned flight (the *Discovery*, on September 29, 1988).

Improvement in the United States economy

In the April 1993 issue of *Fate* magazine, Vaughan predicted, "The U.S. economy will strongly improve the second half of the year. The GNP will grow about 5.4 percent for the year." In a reply to the author on February 23, 1998, Vaughan commented, "The economy improved far more than economists had forecast and came in almost exactly to my predicted figure."

Russian demonstrations against Boris Yeltsin

Also in the April 1993 issue of *Fate* magazine, Vaughan predicted, "In Russia, Boris Yeltsin will face a demonstration against his government in the fall. There will be some casualties." Yeltsin had survived an impeachment attempt in March, but he received strong support from voters in April of that year. However, in September he dissolved Parliament, which in turn deposed him. In the fall as predicted, specifically on October 3, Yeltsin ordered the army to seize the Parliament building, which his political enemies had broken into and were controlling. About 140 people were killed and 150 were arrested. It was the most violent demonstration the country had seen in fifty years.

Mars probe

In January of 1997, Vaughan predicted that the Mars probe scheduled to land six months from then—on July 4— would stop transmitting as it got close to Mars. His prediction was aired in February on the television program *Strange Universe*. Indeed, serious communication problems surrounding the probe started in early July.

Vaughan on His Own Predictions

In 1980, *The Book of Predictions* by David Wallechinsky, Amy Wallace, and Irving Wallace included a dozen of Vaughan's predictions. The ones that are considered accurate are listed below and are paired with Vaughan's 1997 comments on the predictions. All are listed in chronological order of the year associated with each prediction.

1980: "By mid-1982 the inflation rate in the United States will subside to 8 percent."
1997: "Happened exactly as predicted."

1980: "In 1984 the U.S. will start a massively funded program in psychic research in an attempt to catch up with Soviet advances. Like the Soviet program, the American psychic program will be developed by the military."
1997: "This proved to be true. Several books in 1984 described it and now more is coming out about the secret American military program, such as described in David Morehouse's *Psychic Warrior*."

1980: "In 1987 holographic television will be introduced on a limited basis."
1997: This was true. "The Russians did it first," Vaughan commented.

1980: "In 1989 nuclear weapons will be outlawed. U.S. and U.S.S.R. stockpiles will be disarmed."
1997: "The Soviet Union collapsed in 1989 and nuclear weapons stockpiles are being disarmed. For instance, the Americans are now helping Ukranians disarm their stockpiles."

These can be considered partially accurate:

1980: "Between 1982 and 1994 there will be a series of small, conventional wars and skirmishes in the Near East, bringing into being a new country comprised of Sunni Muslims. The Shiite Muslim population will be confined to part of what is now Iran."

1997: "There were wars between the different types of Muslims in Iran and Iraq but no new nation was formed."

1980: "In 1984 the U.S. will introduce an International World Games in Los Angeles to replace the Olympics."

1997: "Ted Turner introduced a new world games, but it did not replace the Olympics."

1980: "In 1990 there will be a drastic devaluation of U.S. currency overnight.... New currency will be printed."

1997: "There was no devaluation. New currency was designed but never put in circulation."

1980: "In 1991 gas-powered automobiles will be banned from metropolitan areas in the U.S., Europe, and Japan. Battery-powered autos will become standard in city areas."

1997: "Battery-powered autos are only now being introduced in Los Angeles, with a mandate that they constitute at least 10 percent of autos in the next few years."

However, Vaughan's predictions about the following events have not come true for any date, as yet.

✧ "In 1987 genetic engineering will develop a gas-producing sea organism to provide enormous amounts of methane for energy production."

✧ "In 1990 a prototype electrosolar satellite will collect energy from the sun and beam it to earth."

✧ "In 1992 the first manned flight to Mars will benefit
   from a vastly improved propulsion system based on anti-
   gravity principles."
✧ "By 1993 electrosolar satellites will have a large impact
   on energy problems."

Vaughan is quite honest about his failure to predict these
events, admitting in an interview that these and other events
"never happened," or "haven't happened as predicted yet."
Still, his accuracy down to small details on so many different
subjects makes him well deserving of the growing interest
surrounding his work.

Predictions Contained in Dreams

While living in Brooklyn from 1969 to 1972, Vaughan worked
as a subject in dream telepathy experiments at Maimonides,
in Brooklyn. He wrote a book on this research, called *Dream
Telepathy*, which he co-authored with Montague Ullman and
Stanley Krippner. Here, Vaughan successfully demonstrated
his own gift for this type of telepathy by dreaming about
photos or illustrations that someone was concentrating on in
another building. He also dreamed about future real-life
events, both at the lab and at home. A detailed dream he
reported in 1969 about a Caribbean search for lost ships, for
example, was later thought to have been a premonition about
a 1985 Jamaican research project to locate two of Christopher
Columbus's lost ships, which had been broken to pieces and
swept out to sea by tidal waves. Eighty-six percent of
Vaughan's psychic statements on this project, undertaken by
the Mobius Society in Los Angeles, were rated accurate
"hits." (The Mobius Society develops "consensus prediction"
in archaeology; criminal investigations, including murder
cases; psychic healing; and remote viewing.) Similarly,
Vaughan's 1977 dream of a voyage in the Indian Ocean

apparently came true seventeen years later in 1994, when an expedition in that area was conducted to find a sunken treasure ship. He believes this to be the farthest he has seen into the future using dream telepathy.

A Prophet in Demand

From 1973 to 1977 Vaughan served as the editor of *Psychic* magazine in San Francisco. The book *Psychics* (1972), which Vaughan edited, was a compilation of interviews with famous mediums from his days at *Psychic* magazine. His own interviews with psychics Arthur Ford, Irene Hughes, and Douglas Johnson appeared in that book.

Since 1980, Vaughan has worked in Los Angeles as a professional intuitive, a channeler, an editor of *Reincarnation Report*, a psychic seminar trainer, and a co-developer of intuition-training software, which he calls "Psychic Reward." According to Vaughan, "It successfully trains people to improve their ability to both predict the future and make it happen." He is now developing a simpler hand-held version of the software called "Psychic Roulette." Vaughan also acts as a psychic consultant for the Mobius Society.

Helping the police

In 1981, police in Lancaster, Pennsylvania, reported that a fourteen-year-old girl was missing. When he was handed a photo of the girl in Los Angeles, Vaughan accurately described how she had been murdered. He gave a description of the murderer, his car, and how far he lived from the girl's house. Police then found the body and the murderer, who was convicted and is now serving a life sentence. District Attorney Mick Rank said that Vaughan's psychic statements were 85 percent correct. A made-for-television movie about the case was in development at the time this book was published.

Channeling spirit guide Li Sung

Vaughan's work in channeling began in 1983 when, after teaching the first day of a psychic seminar, a couple asked him about their past lives. Vaughan spontaneously went into a trance. A Chinese entity named Li Sung spoke through him, giving details not only of the couple's present life but also of a past life the two shared. Later, the couple confirmed that Vaughan, as Li Sung, had accurately described details of their current life. From then on, Vaughan has channeled Li Sung at will. The coming of Li Sung was not a surprise to Vaughan: In 1967 three British mediums predicted he would channel this entity, whom they even mentioned by name. Vaughan has since channeled guidance, sometimes given by Li Sung, for thousands of people, including television personality David Susskind.

According to Vaughan, Li Sung taught him healing and psychic reading of past lives. In a healing experiment for Mobius, Vaughan and Li Sung were able to "dematerialize" a patient's painful kidney stone, as shown by new X-rays. On another occasion, they obtained the same results by using psychic powers on a hospital patient's gallstones. And, a past-life reading gave instant relief to a person suffering from a pain over his heart, which had baffled many doctors.

Looking for buried treasure

In 1987, explorers undertook a project to locate a Spanish treasure ship buried somewhere in the Bahamas. Vaughan predicted that it would take seven years to find it. In 1994, seven years later, the ship was found near Bimini in the Bahamas by Rick Meyer, who claimed it was a Spanish galleon named *Santiago El Grande*. However, Vaughan notes, "Others, including myself, dispute that a ship of that name ever existed. But whatever ship it is, it did yield emeralds and gold coins. Further digging has been hampered by a record number of hurricanes in that area."

Continuing Research and Publications

In 1977 Vaughan received an honorary doctorate in parapsychology from a Spanish institute for his chapter on psychics in *Psychic Exploration*, edited by Edgar Mitchell and John White. Vaughan's research on precognition was published in *Patterns of Prophecy* (1973), *The Edge of Tomorrow* (1982), and *The Power of Positive Prophecy* (1991). Vaughan earned a doctorate in therapeutic counseling in 1993 from the Open International University in Sri Lanka for work he had done at the International Institute of Integral Human Sciences in Montreal.

He currently is working on two books: a biography of medium Eileen Garrett (1893–1970) and an investigation into the possibility of alien presence. Vaughan says the alien presence book "will have a testable hypothesis, which links ESP [extrasensory perception] and alien visitation to other dimensions and geomagnetism."

Vaughan Creates His Destiny

Vaughan's experience with prophecy has led him to believe that "We are born with our chosen destiny." In *The Power of Positive Prophecy*, he sums up what he has found to be the core of most religious thought on this point. "Created in the image of God, we are not only endowed with His powers, but also His destiny: to create our own universes, to discover our inner destiny and fulfill it by prophesying and creating our future."

Keeping an open mind

Most of the prophets profiled in this book stayed with one type of psychic phenomena or power, or combined a few, such as healing and clairvoyance. Vaughan appears to be ever expanding his horizons, exploring many different areas of the psychic realm. For example, he did experimental work in psychokinesis—the ability to move physical objects using only the mind, by affecting magnetic fields—at SRI International. Probably the most famous practitioner of psychokinesis is Uri Geller, who has been televised bending forks and other objects by sheer "brainpower."

Vaughan has developed his own theories that do not always correspond to other prophets' most adamant beliefs. When asked his opinion on Edgar Cayce's axis-tilting prophecies, for example, his answer was good news for humankind.

"My own channeled guidance on this topic," Vaughan replied, "says that the blueprint of catastrophe has been changed—that contemporary prophets who foresee worldwide disasters are reading an out-of-date akashic record. The predicted earth changes have been softened and made much more gradual, averting sudden catastrophe."

With such a well-rounded and accurate prophet as Alan Vaughan among us now, it will be interesting to see what he has to say as we enter a new millennium.

BIBLE PROPHETS

I will stand upon my watch, and set me upon the tower, and will watch to see what he will say unto me, and what I shall answer when I am reproved.

And the Lord answered me, and said, Write the vision, and make it plain upon tables, that he may run that readeth it.

— Hab 2: 1–2 KJV

In the Bible, primarily in the Old Testament, prophets were God's messengers called to be his voice and spread his word. In fiery and eloquent language they railed against worshiping false gods, sin, and wayward living. Most were sent by God to warn the people of Israel against breaking their covenant with him. Some were sent to see God's chosen people through times of exile and suffering. Others preached a message of hope—of God's forgiveness, the coming of a Messiah, and the final triumph of good over evil at the time of the apocalypse. For those who were faithful, these prophets inspired hope and loyalty; for those who weren't, they brought warnings of plagues, destruction, and death.

Rather than predicting events far in the future, most biblical prophets referred to events specific to their own people, which were likely to happen during their own lifetimes. Thus, their vision serves as a window into early biblical times, especially into the continual political strife in the holy lands. The accuracy of their "predictions," a term that must here be used loosely, is almost impossible to verify, for two reasons. First, because their words, thoughts, and deeds weren't written down in the Bible until long after most of the events they predicted had taken place, some have argued that biblical authors conveniently filled in details to make it appear as though the prophets had forecast the future, whether or not they actually had. Second, because one of the prophets' most important functions was to warn people against wrongdoing, much of what they preached was simply what God could be expected to do if people continued to defy him. Their warnings didn't necessarily translate into specific predictions.

Though such prophets exist in most religions, this chapter focuses on mainstream prophets within the Judeo-Christian tradition, specifically on the major and minor prophets of the Hebrew Bible, or Old Testament. Another category of Bible prophecy, called apocalyptic literature, is also briefly touched on here. The Book of Revelation in the New Testament is the most widely recognized of these writings that deal with the apocalypse, or the end of time.

Biblical prophets are usually classified as "major" or "minor," which refers to the length of the books attributed to them, not to their particular significance in the grand scheme of things. The major prophets include Isaiah, Jeremiah, Ezekiel, and Daniel. The minor prophets are Hosea, Joel, Amos, Obadiah, Jonah, Micah, Nahum, Habakkuk, Zephaniah, Haggai, Zechariah, and Malachi.

While some prophetic books were thought to be written by the prophets themselves, it is more likely that their teachings were passed on from the prophets' disciples to ancient scribes who actually wrote down the works for posterity.

All the prophetical books, with the exception of Jonah, present the lives and messages of oracles speaking in poetic language against the evils both within Israel and in foreign countries. Jonah, on the other hand, tells the story of a prophet, not the words of God spoken through a prophet.

This chapter briefly describes each prophet's most significant teachings or predictions. While an attempt was made to present these prophets chronologically, it is difficult to guarantee the exact order of events, as scholars still debate the actual dating of most biblical literature. The editors of this book have chosen to use the King James Version of the Bible for quotations cited in this chapter.

Amos

Amos was the first of the "writing" prophets, which means he was believed to be the first prophet to have written his own book of the Bible. He was a champion of the poor, known for speaking out against social injustice and the hypocrisy he believed was rampant among the leaders of Israel.

Amos, who was a humble shepherd, lived in the southern kingdom of Judah between 787 and 742 B.C. At first he resisted God's calling, saying, "I am no prophet, nor a prophet's son; but I am a herdsman." However, Amos became resigned to his destiny: "The Lord took me from following the flock, and the Lord said to me, 'Go, prophesy to my people Israel'" (Amos 7:14–15).

Amos faced several challenges. His message was often addressed to the rich and powerful, yet he was only a shepherd. He was from the southern kingdom of Judah, yet his ministry and his message was directed at the central royal sanctuary of Bethlehem in the kingdom of Israel. As God's mouthpiece, Amos threatened punishments in the form of exile, death, and destruction for the citizens of the powerful nation of Israel who were responsible for exploiting the poor, saying that King Jeroboam II would die by the sword (Amos 7:11). He preached that God's judgment was near at hand, but because the times were prosperous, many resisted his gloomy message. Moreover, Amos spoke out against social injustice, which he observed in the great gap between the rich leaders and the poor common folk. Not surprisingly, he was expelled from the sanctuary and forbidden to preach there.

In the final section of the book of Amos, the Lord speaks through the prophet: "In that day I will raise up the booth of David that is fallen and repair its breaches, and raise up its ruins, and rebuild it as in the days of old...." (Amos 9:11). Because these verses predicting the restoration of the line of David are in a style uncharacteristic of the rest of the book, experts generally believe that these lines were added by another writer at a later date. In any case, the line of David was restored, of course—Jesus was born of this lineage.

Amos also predicted a revolt or war between the classes. He spoke of a glorious age to follow, with the "restoration of the fortunes of my people Israel."

Hosea

The prophet Hosea warned that Israel's rejection of the Lord will bring punishment to the people, including the loss of everything: leadership, children, places of worship, and even country.

In Scripture, Hosea's warnings to the people about their faithlessness are played out symbolically with his divinely commanded marriage to Gomer, a "wife of harlotry." The details of his marriage serve as a metaphor for Israel's broken covenant with the Lord. Hosea's book is filled with accusations of whoredom.

"My people ask counsel at their stocks, and their staff declareth unto them: for the spirit of whoredoms hath caused *them* to err, and they have gone a whoring from under their God" (Hos. 4:12).

In spite of this strong language, most experts agree that the prophet stresses the theme of divine compassion for the chosen people, not only after they fail but even *as* they fail.

Isaiah

Isaiah, the first prophet to write of the coming of a Messiah, is thought by many to be the greatest of the Old Testament prophets. Like Amos, another eighth-century B.C. prophet, he decried social injustice and religious hypocrisy; but unlike Amos, he thought that rich and poor alike practiced idolatry and other forms of worship not focused on the one true God. Isaiah believed he was called to warn of the judgment that would befall all who turned away from God. He was a passionate advocate of righteous living, which he believed to be a truer form of worship than verbal proclamations of faith. During a time of political and military tensions between neighboring lands, Isaiah urged the people to rely on God alone to protect Israel.

Almost nothing is known of Isaiah's early life, except that he was the son of a man named Amoz. According to his own words, Isaiah had a profound vision of God when he was in his mid-twenties, and from that day on he devoted himself to prophesying. A distinguished citizen of Jerusalem, he was considered an outstanding poet, writer, and statesman. He led a fairly normal life with his wife and two sons and evidently was respected by those who knew him.

Some of the most familiar and beautiful phrases of all Scripture are found in Isaiah, not all of which are actually attributed to the prophet.

"They shall beat their swords into plowshares, and their spears into pruning hooks; nation shall not lift up sword against nation, neither shall they learn war any more" (Isa. 2:4).

"Behold, a virgin shall conceive and bear a son, and shall call his name Immanuel" (Isa. 7:14).

"For unto us, a child is born, unto us a son is given: and the government shall be upon his shoulder: and his name shall be called Wonderful, Counselor, the mighty God, the Everlasting Father, the Prince of Peace" (Isa. 9:6).

"They that wait upon the Lord shall renew their strength; they shall mount up with wings as eagles; they shall run, and not be weary, and they shall walk, and not faint" (Isa. 40:31).

Micah

The events surrounding this prophet from Judea took place from between 750–722 B.C., the same period in which Hosea and Isaiah flourished. Like many other biblical prophets, Micah spoke out against idol worship and social injustice, and warned the Israelites of God's judgment on those who disobeyed.

Micah, like many other prophets, refers to the birth of a King of Peace in Bethlehem: "... yet out of thee shall he come forth unto me that is to be ruler in Israel; whose goings forth have been from of old, from everlasting" (Mic. 5:2).

Jonah

The prophet Jonah, from Galilee, son of Amittai, was born in a town just north of Nazareth. He served as a prophet during the reign of Jeroboam II, between the years 786 and 746 B.C.

In the Bible, God uses Jonah not as his mouthpiece, but more as an example for others to follow. When the Lord called him to prophesy against the wrongdoings of the citizens of Nineveh, capital of Assyria, Jonah was troubled. He feared that if the people of Nineveh listened to him and repented, God would forgive them, and his prediction of their destruction would not come about. So, he disobeyed God's command and tried to flee on a ship bound for Tarshish. God sent a mighty tempest that threatened the lives of all aboard.

Knowing someone must be to blame, the ship's crew cast lots (an ancient form of divination) that pointed to Jonah as the cause of the storm. Jonah told the men to throw him into the sea. There, as the well-known tale goes, he was swallowed by a giant fish, and prayed for God's forgiveness. Three days later he was released onto dry land. This story is commonly thought to be symbolic of the three days during which Jesus was in the tomb before he resurrected.

After this, God told Jonah once again to go to Nineveh. This time, Jonah obeyed, and the people heard his warning and pledged to stop their transgressions. When God then relented and said that he would not punish them, Jonah was angry. God then taught him a lesson: Just as Jonah had been spared, the people of Nineveh also deserved a second chance.

Jonah's story is a good example of how the responsibility of being a prophet was not always easy to shoulder. And in this case, God was able to send a message to the people through example, rather than through words alone.

Zephaniah

Zephaniah lived during the reign of Josiah (640–609 B.C). He preached a message of God's judgment on all those in Jerusalem and elsewhere who had fallen from grace, as well as on those who had never believed in him. "Hold thy peace at the presence of the Lord God, for the day of the Lord is at hand: for the Lord hath prepared a sacrifice, he hath bid his guests," Zephaniah told his people (Zeph.1:7). He also described the day of the Lord as one of wrath and darkness, and he foresaw that his nation would fall into the hands of an unknown invader. He declared that the righteous would eventually return from captivity, however, and sing for joy.

Nahum

Like Jonah, the prophet Nahum foretold the destruction of Nineveh, the ancient capital of Assyria, now located in northern Iraq. In describing how Nineveh would fall, Nahum's language comes remarkably close to what actually happened. "The gates of the river shall be opened, and the palace shall be dissolved" (Nah. 2:6), he says. In 612 B.C., shortly after Nahum had made this proclamation, an alliance between the Medes, Babylonians, and Scythians unleashed the Khoser River into Nineveh, causing flooding that eroded the bricks of the city's buildings.

Nahum's prophecies built up Jerusalem's hopes of acquiring greater political power, but Jerusalem fell shortly after Nineveh to the Babylonians, the new power in the Middle East before the Persians took their place.

The book of Nahum presents God (Yahweh) as telling the people of Israel, through Nahum, of the punishments that will befall them if they do not repent. "Behold, I am against thee, saith the Lord of Hosts: I will burn her chariots in the smoke, and the sword shall devour thy young lions ..." (Nah. 2:13).

Jeremiah

Jeremiah, who has been called "the weeping prophet" for his gloomy predictions, also has been identified as one of the most Christlike figures in the Bible because of his long-suffering nature and unshakeable faith. His book of the Bible is one of the most autobiographical of any of the prophets, giving readers much insight into his life and times. Jeremiah's prophecies concerned the reigns of the last five kings of Judah, and like many other prophets, he warned that God would punish those who practiced sin and idolatry.

This long book of fifty-two chapters includes hundreds of specific prophecies, many predicting the triumph of the Jews over their enemies, such as the Babylonians: "Though Babylon should mount up to heaven, and though she should fortify the height of her strength, yet from them shall spoilers come unto her, saith the Lord" (Jer. 51:53).

One of the most important messages of the prophecy of Jeremiah is that contact with God must be personal, even intimate. Jeremiah's testimony can be viewed as a preparation for the incarnation of God in the person of Jesus.

Habakkuk

Habakkuk was a prophet during the reigns of Jehoiakiam and Josia, from about 612 to 597 B.C. He was a contemporary of Jeremiah who lived somewhat later than Nahum. Unlike other prophets, Habakkuk seemed at times to doubt God's actions, and asked God to explain the presence of evil in the world. Habakkuk was plagued by troubling questions. Why does God allow suffering? Why does evil go unpunished? He said, "O Lord, how long shall I cry, and thou wilt not hear! Even cry out unto thee of violence, and thou wilt not save! Why dost thou show me iniquity, and cause me to behold grievance? For spoiling and violence are before me ..." (Hab. 1:2-3).

Habakkuk was concerned that when the Babylonians conquered Nineveh and ousted the evil King Jehoiakim, they also would rule in tyranny. He was answered by a vision of God in which God caused the ground to tremble, drove nations "asunder," and scattered the mountains to save his people. This vision convinced Habakkuk to put his absolute trust and faith in the Lord.

Daniel

Daniel, the son of a wealthy merchant, was captured when he was just a boy and exiled to pagan Babylon in the sixth century B.C. When he was in training to be one of King Nebuchadnezzar's courtiers, it was discovered that he could interpret the king's dreams. Strangely, he could not interpret his own dreams; when he attempted to do so, he became weak and sick. Later, his dreams were interpreted for him by angels, including the angel Gabriel. He was known for being godly and wise, and he was much sought after for the insights he gained through dreams and visions.

Daniel lived in an era of great persecution (605–536 B.C.). The times influenced his writing, which is filled with promises of better days ahead after the destruction of his nation's enemies.

Stories from the Bible show Daniel to be an accurate prophet. When the disagreeable Babylonian King Belshazzar decided to give a grand feast, he ordered sacred vessels from the Jewish temple to be brought out so the guests could drink from them. After this profane act, a disembodied hand appeared and wrote a message on the wall. The frightened king called on astrologers and enchanters to interpret the act. Daniel told the king that it was a message from God. "This is the interpretation of the thing...God hath numbered thy kingdom, and finished it....Thou art weighed in the balances, and art found wanting....Thy kingdom is divided, and given to the Medes and Persians" (Dan. 5:25–30). The king was slain that night. Babylon was later taken by Darius the Mede, according to the book of Daniel. However, scholars now believe this Darius to be a composite of several rulers created by the author of the book of Daniel.

According to the Bible, Daniel became governor of Babylon as a result of his successful interpretations and visions. However, Darius was persuaded by Daniel's enemies to pass a law that no one could pray to anyone but himself for a month. Daniel, ever loyal to God, continued to pray to the Lord three times a day. Though he didn't want to, Darius was forced to punish him by throwing him into a lions' den. God spared Daniel by "shutting the lions' mouths," which became the tale Daniel is most known for today.

The ten stories in the book of Daniel comprise the first major work of apocalyptic prophecies, or those that tell of upcoming crises and the ultimate victory of good over evil. These set a model for subsequent works, including I Enoch, Syriac, and Baruch, as well as the Book of Revelation. At least indirectly, they may have influenced all prophets thereafter—even secular prophets—in style, if not in substance.

Daniel sent a message of comfort and hope for eternal life, which would be given to people after the establishment of God's final kingdom.

Ezekiel

Between 593 and 563 B.C., a priest named Ezekiel spoke out against idolatry and impurity, and, most importantly, foretold the fall of Jerusalem. His sayings have been rewritten and expanded upon, resulting in a text that Bible scholars believe was harmed in the process. Even so, the book of Ezekiel contains the most thorough chronology of any of the prophetic books. Experts find only two or three dates out of order.

Ezekiel is believed to have been one of those deported to Babylon during the *golah*, or exile, spurred by King Nebuchadnezzar II's takeover of Jerusalem. This group of deported citizens was made up of Jerusalem's prominent families, so it is likely that he was a well-known and well-respected priest. The book of Ezekiel portrays him as prone to strange ecstatic visions and speechlessness. He delivered his messages more like sermons than prophecies, and he was known to use many allegories and to emphasize the importance of ritual.

Ezekiel's first calling to prophesy was particularly dramatic. According to the Bible (Authorized King James Version), God came to him as a vision, first as a great whirlwind out of the north. This changed to a fire, in which Ezekiel beheld the color of amber. In the midst of this fire, four strange creatures emerged. Each had four heads, four faces (of a man, a lion, an ox, and an eagle), and four wings, and they were joined together. These creatures reminded him of wheels within wheels, among other things; and finally he was struck once more by the presence of amber. Ezekiel fell to his knees, and the Lord spoke to him.

"And he said unto me, Son of man, I send thee to the children of Israel, to a rebellious nation that hath rebelled against me, even unto this very day.

"For they are impudent children and stiffhearted. I do send thee unto them; and thou shalt say unto them, Thus saith the Lord God.

"And they, whether they will hear, or whether they will forbear (for they are a rebellious house), yet shall know that there hath been a prophet among them" (Ezek. 2:3–5).

Later God told him, "Son of man, I have made thee a watchman unto the house of Israel; therefore hear the word at my mouth, and give them warning from me" (Ezek. 2:17).

Ezekial's warnings to the people of Israel for turning away from God were quite specific.

"A third part of thee shall die with the pestilence, and with famine shall they be consumed in the midst of thee and a third part shall fall by the sword round about thee; and I will scatter a third part into all the winds, and I will draw out a sword after them" (Ezek. 5:12).

Obadiah

The name Obadiah means "servant of the Lord," and as such is the name of a dozen different people in the Old Testament. Not much is known about the prophet Obadiah, or even about the time period in which he was supposed to have lived. However, in the opening lines of the Book of Obadiah, he is called an ambassador of the Lord, sent among the heathen (Obad. 1:1).

Some of the predictions in this shortest book of the Bible were spoken or written shortly after Jerusalem fell to the Babylonians in the late sixth century B.C. The prophecies are addressed to Edom, southeast of Palestine. The Edomites had celebrated the fall of Jerusalem and imprisoned its refugees. For these actions, Obadiah warns the Edomites that God will destroy them and turn their lands over to Israel.

He tells the Edomites:

"As you have done, it shall be done to you, your deed shall return on your own head" (Obad. 15).

Haggai

Haggai's prophecy appeared to be limited to a very short period of time, August through December in the year 520 B.C. Together with the prophet Zechariah, Haggai was known for encouraging the Israelites to rebuild their temple, which they had neglected in favor of constructing new homes for themselves.

Zechariah

Zechariah's prophecy is dated two months after Haggai's in 520 B.C. He joined Haggai in urging the people to rebuild their temple in Jerusalem, and he focused on the temple as a symbol of Israel. He spoke of the coming of the Messiah and the redemption of Israel.

His messianic prophecy includes details that are borne out in the New Testament. "Rejoice greatly, O daughter of Zion; shout, O daughter of Jerusalem; behold, thy King cometh unto thee: he is just, and having salvation; lowly, and riding upon an ass . . ." (Zech. 9:9).

Many see this as a prophecy or prediction of Jesus' triumphant entry into Jerusalem on what is now known as Palm Sunday. "And Jesus, when he had found a young ass, sat thereon; as it is written, Fear not, daughter of Sion: behold, thy King cometh, sitting on an ass's colt" (John 12:14–15).

Joel

We know little of Joel, though it is possible he was Samuel's first son. There are a dozen other men with that name in the Old Testament. But the prophet may have lived between 539 and 331 B.C. During his lifetime the Persians had allowed the Jews to return to Judah, but times were difficult. Joel believed that the harsh conditions ravaging the country, including a locust plague, fires, and drought, were warning signs from God.

"Blow ye the trumpet in Zion, and sound an alarm in my holy mountain: let all the inhabitants of the land tremble: for the day of the Lord cometh, for it is nigh at hand" (Joel 2:1).

Joel called for the people to come pray and repent at the temple. In return, he told them, God promised to stop the scourges and save the people from their enemies.

Malachi

The events in the book of Malachi were thought to have occurred around 430 B.C. As a book of the Bible, Malachi served the important function of reinforcing other prophets' visions of the coming of the Messiah. Scholars are not convinced, however, that a real person by that name existed. It is likely that this book was written anonymously. Nonetheless, the voice of this book urged the Israelites to keep God's commandments, pay tithes, and believe in the promise of God's mercy.

A key passage in the book is: "Behold, I will send you Elijah the prophet before the coming of the great and dreadful day of the Lord" (Mal. 4:5). In the New Testament, Matthew 11:13 refers to this passage, and to Elijah as St. John the Baptist.

The book of Malachi brings the Old Testament to a close, with more predictions about the coming of Elijah, whom many consider to have been John the Baptist: "Know that I am going to send you Elijah the prophet before my day comes, that great and terrible day. He shall turn the heart of fathers towards their children and the heart of children towards their fathers lest I come and smite the earth with a curse" (Mal. 4:5–6).

New Testament Prophecy

Prophecy was not solely the domain of the Old Testament. The most outstanding examples of New Testament prophets are Jesus himself; John the Baptist; and John, author of The Book of Revelation.

Both Jesus and John the Baptist, whose births were foretold by many Old Testament prophets, were Judaic prophets in their own rights: individuals chosen by God to reveal to the people God's intentions—bearers of a divine revelation or warning who received the strength to communicate God's word, while accepting that to do so would mean persecution, suffering, and even death.

John the Baptist was a cousin of Jesus. At the age of about thirty, he began preaching in the wilderness of Judea about the coming of the Messiah and calling on the people to repent and reform in preparation for the Day of the Lord.

Jesus cited an Old Testament prophecy in declaring the truth of his own mission to the nation of Israel:

"The woman said to him, 'I know that Messiah is coming' (who is called Christ). 'When he comes, he will proclaim all things to us.' Jesus said to her, 'I am he, the one who is speaking to you' (John 4:25–26 NRSV)."

Jesus also prophesied his own persecution, death, and resurrection, as the fulfillment of messianic prophecy:

And Jesus going up to Jerusalem took the twelve disciples apart in the way, and said unto them,

"Behold, we go up to Jerusalem; and the son of man shall be betrayed unto the chief priests and unto the scribes, and they shall condemn him to death,

And shall deliver him to the Gentiles to mock, and to scourge, and to crucify him: and the third day he shall rise again" (Matt. 20:17–19).

At the Last Supper, Jesus foretold the exact manner in which his betrayal would unfold, as well as the actions of key disciples during the crucial days and hours directly following the crucifixion:

Now when the even was come, he sat down with the twelve.

And as they did eat, he said, "Verily I say unto you, that one of you shall betray me" (Matt. 26:20–21).

But Peter said unto him, "Although all shall be offended, yet will not I."

And Jesus saith unto him, "Verily I say unto thee, that this day, even in this night, before the cock crow twice, thou shalt deny me thrice" (Mark 14:29–30).

All of these prophecies came to pass in short order and reinforced the believers' faith in Jesus as the promised Messiah.

The Book of Revelation

The Book of Revelation, written in rich allegorical language, is the last book of the New Testament and its only prophetic book. It contains a series of predictive visions of the struggles—and ultimate victory through God's intervention—of the Christian Church over both internal and external forces of opposition. This book is sometimes called The Apocalypse. Both titles in English are derived from *apokalypsis*, the first word in the Greek original, which means "revelation."

In general, apocalyptic writing features a revelation from God about future events that are delivered to a prophet through a divine intermediary. In the Book of Revelation, Jesus Christ is the go-between: "I Jesus have sent mine angel to testify unto you these things in the churches. I am the root and the offspring of David, and the bright and morning star" (Rev. 22:16).

The author and seer is John, an early Christian writer. "In the spirit on the Lord's day," John heard "a great voice, as of a trumpet" (Rev. 1:10), which told him to record what he would see in a vision and send that to the seven churches of

Ephesus, Smyrna, Pergamum, Thyatira, Sardis, Philadelphia, and Laodicea in preparation for what was to come. John receives seven highly symbolic visions that tell the story of the Christian Church from its beginnings to the end of the existing world. All that John is shown, he records in rich detail that is as terrifying in its intensity as it is awe-inspiring in its language and mysticism.

Scholars believe that the writing of Revelation took place on Patmos, a Dodecanese island in the Aegean Sea where John the Evangelist was banished during the reign of the Roman emperor, either Vespasian (A.D. 69 to 79) or Domitian (A.D. 81 to 96), for preaching "the word of God, and for the testimony of Jesus Christ" (Rev. 1:9).

The author's writing style is derived from the prophetic books of the Old Testament as well as from oral tradition, and alludes frequently to Old Testament prophecy, especially that of Ezekiel, Daniel, and Isaiah. The highly developed use of such literary devices as allegory, imagery, and animal and numerical symbolism concealed Revelation's message from enemies of the church. Although the book was most likely understood by early Christian readers, many of the keys to decoding Revelation's symbolism have been lost over the centuries, leaving it open to widely differing interpretations in every era of Christianity.

The Christians of the first century believed that evil in the world would increase and intensify. Furthermore, they believed that God's intervention was close at hand and would be followed by a new age in which Christ and the church and its martyrs would be triumphant. The persecution that Christians endured at that time at the hands of the Romans appeared to be a signal that the final cataclysm had begun. The letters to the seven churches, which form the opening chapters of the Book of Revelation, offer both warnings and encouragement for the battles to come. The final chapters offer the promise of a triumphant age of eternal justice.

And I saw a new heaven and a new earth: for the first heaven and earth were passed away; and there was no more sea.

And I John saw the holy city, new Jerusalem, coming down from God out of heaven, prepared as a bride adorned for her husband (Rev. 21:1–2).

And God shall wipe away all tears from their eyes; and there shall be no more death, neither sorrow, nor crying, neither shall there be any more pain: for the former things are passed away (Rev. 21:4).

Today, the Book of Revelation is valued as much for its extraordinary literary qualities as for its record of crises in early Christianity, its help in understanding the ills that plague our world, and the prophecy of the everlasting kingdom of God on earth that many believe is still to come.

Suggested Readings

The following books, except for those that are indicated with an asterisk (*), are available on the Internet through www.amazon.com. Books not listed in amazon.com might be in other bookstores or in used bookstores as listed in www.bibliofind.com. Citations to additional readings may be requested from the author at donwigal@ix.netcom.com.

Books are organized here by chapter topics.

Introduction

Brown, Michael. *The Channeling Zone: American Spirituality in an Anxious Age.* Cambridge: Harvard University Press, 1997.
See also interview with author on-line in amazon.com.

Garrett, Eileen J. *The Sense and Nonsense of Prophecy.* New York: Creative Age Press, 1950.*
Chapter 15 on cult leaders is especially helpful.

Guiley, Rosemary Ellen. *Harper's Encyclopedia of Mystical and Paranormal Experience.* San Francisco: Harper Collins, 1991.
A basic reference for personal libraries.

Jung, Carl G. "On Synchronicity," *The Portable Jung.* New York: Viking, 1971. Edited by Joseph Campbell. Pages 508-518.
Gives a better understanding of the Eternal Now, which prophets often say can be accessed.

Mann, A. T. *Millennium Prophecies: Predictions for the Year 2000.* Rockport, Mass.: Element, 1995.
Some information is out-of-date, but otherwise a helpful approach.

Wigal, Donald. *The Best Guide to the Unexplained*. Los Angeles: Renaissance, 1998.
See chapter on prophecy.

Leonardo da Vinci

Freud, Sigmund. *Leonardo da Vinci, a Study in Psychosexuality*. Translated by A. A. Brill. New York: Random House, 1947.*
A seminal work of the genre that reveals more about Freud than Leonardo.

Whiting, Roger. *Leonardo: A Portrait of the Renaissance Man*. London, England: Barrie & Jenkins, 1992.
See chapter 9: "The Civil Engineer and Inventor."

Nostradamus

Cheetam, Erika. *The Final Prophecies of Nostradamus*. London, England: Futura, 1990.

King, Francis X. *Nostradamus: Prophecies Fulfilled and Predictions for the Millennium & Beyond*. New York: St. Martin's Press, 1994.
An entertaining coffee-table book approach.

LeVert, Liberté E. *The Prophecies and Enigmas of Nostradamus*. Glen Rock, N.J., 1997.*

Paulus, Stefan. *Nostradamus 1999: Who Will Survive?* St. Paul: Llewelyn, 1997.
For some interesting insights, read the author's note at the end of the book first.

Randi, James. *The Mask of Nostradamus: The Prophecies of the World's Most Famous Seer*. Buffalo, N.Y.: Prometheus Books, 1993.
The best of the skeptics' books about Nostradamus. See the summary of Randi's knowledge of paranormal phenomena on page 54.

John Dee

James, Geoffrey. *The Enochian Magic of John Dee.* St. Paul: Llewellyn, 1997.
This is one of several unique books on the truly bizarre from Llewellyn.

Randi, James. "Contemporary Seers," *The Mask of Nostradamus.* Buffalo, N.Y.: Prometheus Books, 1993.

Schueler, Gerald and Betty.
There are at least six books by these experts that apply Dee's Enochian Magic to physics, the Tarot, religious rites, or even four-player chess. Search amazon.com on the Internet or see the catalog of Llewellyn Publications, St. Paul, MN 55164-0383.

Kenneth Mackenzie

Stewart, Robb. *Strange Prophecies that Came True.* New York: Ace, 1987.*
See pages 128–130.

Jules Verne

Haining, Peter. *The Jules Verne Companion.* London, England: Souvenir Press, 1978.

Verne, Jean-Jules. *Jules Verne.* London, England: Taplinger, 1976. *

Andrew Jackson Davis

Beaver, Harold. *The Science Fiction of Edgar Allan Poe.* New York: Penguin, 1976.*
See "Eureka: An Essay on the Material and Spiritual Universe" and "Mellonta Tauta."

Evangeline Adams

Wallechinsky, David and Irving Wallace. *The People's Almanac Presents The Book of Predictions.* New York: William Morrow, 1981.
See page 363. This work is hard to find. *

Edgar Cayce

Stearn, Jess. *Edgar Cayce: The Sleeping Prophet.* New York: Bantam, 1967.

Timms, Moira. *Beyond Prophecies and Predictions: Everyone's Guide to the Coming Change.* New York: Ballentine, 1994.
See chapter 3: "Cosmic cycles"; chapter 4: "Astrological cycles."

Wallechinsky, David and Irving Wallace. *The People's Almanac Presents The Book of Predictions.* New York: William Morrow, 1981.
Hard to find.*

Jeane Dixon

Dixon, Jeane. *My Life and Prophecies; Her Own Story Told to Rene Noorbergen.* New York: G. K. Hall, 1971.

Randi, James. *The Mask of Nostradamus.* Buffalo, N.Y.: Prometheus Books, 1993.
See the entry for Dixon in the index.

Alan Vaughan

Vaughan, Alan. *Doorways to Higher Consciousness: Opening to the Gifts of Spirit.* Williamsburg, Va.: Celest Press, 1998.

_____ *The Edge of Tomorrow: How to Foresee and Fulfill Your Future.* Santa Fe, N.M.: Sun Publishing, 1997.

_____ (coauthored with M. Ullman and S. Krippner) *Dream Telepathy: Experiences in Nocturnal ESP.* 2nd ed., Jefferson, N.C.: McFarland, 1989.

_____ *Incredible Coincidence: The Baffling World of Synchronicity.* New York, N.Y.: Ballantine, 1989.

_____ *Patterns of Prophecy.* Santa Fe, N.M.: Sun Publishing, 1997.

_____ *The Power of Positive Prophecy; How to Envision and Create Your Future.* London: HarperCollins, 1991.*

_____ *Spiritual Channeling.* VHS Tape. Berkeley, Calif.: Thinking Allowed Productions, 1990.

Bible Prophets

Bells, Alice Ogden. [Editor] *Many Voices: Multicultural Responses to the Minor Prophets.* Lanham, Md.: University Press of America, 1995.*
A unique student project.

Gattey, Charles Nelson. *Prophecy and Prediction in the 20th Century.* San Francisco: HarperCollins, 1990.

Wigal, Donald. *1001 Questions on the Bible.* Amsterdam, N.Y.: Coleco, 1981.*
Daily on-line edition at www.wigal.com.

Prophecy and Intuition

The Alternative Research provides free information on a registry of prophecy. Send a self-addressed, stamped envelope to:

The Alternative Research
Box 432
New York, NY 10156

ACKNOWLEDGMENTS

The author wishes to thank Judy Curtis of the Adams National Historical Museum; The Abigail Adams Smith Museum; Antoni Bautista from the *New York Times*; Stuart Dean of the Association for Research and Enlightenment; Linda Bussaca of Columbia University; the Jimmy Carter Library; Bonnie Crellin of the New School for Social Research; Cathleen Saraceni of the Carnegie Hall Archives; Edi Hanson; James Hewitt, Ph.D.; Sharon Hymer, Ph.D.; Vera Haldy-Reiger; Paul Levy at the Jung Center; the Ronald Reagan Library; Dorothy Dumond of the Klyne Esopus Clerical Society Museum; John Fitzgerald Kennedy Library; Karen Christina Kraar; William Kuhns for ongoing advice and the generous loan of his extensive library; Elizabeth Loree; Corey Malcum; Mairena Montoya; Irene Kennedy of The Museum of the City of New York; The Museum of Science in Boston; New York Historical Society; Barbara Nixon; Richard Nixon Library and Birthplace; The New York City Public Library reference desk; Kay O'Reilly; C. J. Puotinen and Joel Hollenberg; James Robert Parish, who first proposed me to the publisher; Vanessa Pintado of the Pierpont Morgan Library; George Sullivan; Moira Timms; Alan Vaughan; Norman Winski; and Craig Zraly of Columbia University. Finally, the author and publisher give special thanks to editors Heather Green and Leslie Eckard, designer Janet Little, and illustrator Susan Chamberlain.

Don Wigal, Ph.D.

About The Author

Donald Wigal, Ph.D., co-authored the four-book *Experiences in Faith* series in 1970, shortly after returning to the secular world after seventeen years in a religious order. He holds degrees in music, adult education, and liturgical theology, all of which he has taught at universities, along with Gregorian chant and film education. He also has certifications from the Institute for Spiritual Theology and from the University of the City of New York.

Wigal has written for encyclopedias, including *The Encyclopedia of Mystical and Paranormal Experience*. His books include *1001 Questions About the Bible, General Knowledge*, and *The Best Guide to the Unexplained*. His popular web site (http://www.wigal.com) has for several years included his daily Scripture education program.

In 1985, Wigal was awarded the Distinguished Alumnus Award from the University of Dayton. He is an ASCAP composer and I Ching practitioner.